POETRY IN RHYTHM
By a Glasgow Poet

Eddie Allan

Published by
Super Scot Publications
0 / 2 Peabody Trust
Camberwell Green
London SE5 7BY

Digitally printed by
Intype London Ltd
Units 3-4
Elm Grove Industrial Estate
Elm Grove
London SW19 4HE

Second Edition

A CIP record for this book is available from the British Library

ISBN: 0-9543949-0-9

EDDIE ALLAN WITH LOVE . . .

I dedicate this book to my late mother and father, to my wife's late mother and father, and to other people who are no longer with us who were an inspiration in my Life. I also want to pay tribute to my darling wife and my children, and to my brothers and sisters for giving me encouragement to write this book and so make my dream come true.

CONTENTS

INTRODUCTION

EDDIE, THE MAN

I would like to introduce my childhood friend, Eddie Allan, to the literary world and the common man and woman of his native city, Glasgow, and of his beloved country Scotland. I feel it would be a great shame for the people of Scotland and the people of this globe not to have the privilege to digest this man's poetry. It is funny, sad and in some parts mad and some people would say "bad", but for myself I think it's real and genuine. I also think that within everybody there is a hidden talent.

I became involved with Eddie's poems because every time I went home to Glasgow, this friend Eddie kept asking me to read his work. I knew nothing about poems, but I suppose I was a people pleaser so I took the poetry, not being very interested at the time. I had never read a book from start to finish, until on the train from Glasgow back to London I read this collection of poems. I thought people who read poetry fell into two types. The first lot was of men who wore corduroys and tweed jackets, and smoked pipes. I generally appeared in front of them on the Bench. The second were people who worked at the benefits office, either cutting my benefit or attacking single parents. I didn't know many people who came from Partick, Govan or Yoker or the Clyde in general who were poets. If there were any welders, plumbers or boilermakers from there who had poems published in the paper, I guarantee they would have put them in under a name like Shirley or Jessie.

Eddie is a shy working class ex-shipyard worker, who doesn't have a lot of self-confidence. The part of Glasgow that he came from would be in today's terms classed as socially excluded, it is called Langholme St, Yoker. There people begged, stole or borrowed and worked (when there were jobs). But the Clyde is finished now and the great shipyards and tall cranes are gone.

Most people have heard of Rabbie Burns and Sir Walter Scott. Well, Eddie is not in that category of course, thank God, because he is still alive and well and living with hid wonderful wife Rosemary and six children in Glasgow, and no doubt enjoying life the only way he knows how. He has drunk a lot and smokes like a chimney, he can swear like a trooper but I still think his work is worthy and worthwhile for anyone to look at.

I feel the best compliment I can say about Eddie Allan is that I would have been proud to have had him as a father. I am delighted to introduce him to you the reader, the critic. He is an inspiration to me and it has been a joy and a loving friendship to me personally to be associated with such a vagabond, humorous and loving in his ways, and a loving scoundrel in his heart. Nothing is too much for him to do for you. Try and vision this giant of a man, with a weathered face, and when I mean giant I am not just talking about his stature-I am talking about his heart. So buckle up, sit back and watch the big picture, as you're in for a bumpy ride, as one Hollywood star would say.
I introduce you to my dear friend Edward Allan.

Pat Reilly.

Preface

My name is Eddie Allan. I was born in Anderston, Glasgow, in November 1951, the 7th of 12 kids. I had a very happy childhood, but at age 13, my dad died, aged 47.
I ended up spending a lot of time in institutions.

In 1970 I met Rosemary, whom I married in 1972, three months later our first daughter, Susan, was born. Four months later my mum died, aged 53. we now have 6 kids, from 30 to 9 years of age.

I worked in a variety of jobs, none of which was good for my health. I now have Emphysema, that's why I started writing poems. All of my poems are from personal experiences and events that really strike a chord with me. In 'Alice' I wrote putting myself in the shoes of her husband, Big John. My thoughts are always with him.

All my other poems speak for themselves, and I dedicate each poem to those concerned. I would also like to thank Big Pat and Kevin for all that they have done in getting this book together (God Bless Them). But to my wife and children (and Grandchildren) brothers, sisters, nieces and nephews, and all my friends and acquaintances, this book is really for you.

EDDIE ALLAN

TODAY

I wake up in the morning and think today must be the day
To do the things I want to do no matter what you say
I'll have my day all worked out and think I've got it right
And then I come to realize that it's already night
And I haven't done a single thing that I meant to do
So it's another day that's over, and I'm left here feeling blue
They say tomorrow never comes so I've worked it out this way
I'll do tomorrow all the things I planned to do today
I'll live a life of happiness in all I do or seek
'cause I'll do all I want to do, between now and next week
I'll have the time to do the chores, and even have time for play
The only problem is…
I wont have time for it today.

"WHAT'S UP, DOC?"

You go to see the doctor when you are feeling ill,
The doctor checks you over and prescribes a little pill.
She tells you it will give you some get up and go
What she doesn't tell you is the pill's a placebo.

So when you take the little pill it's not long till you smile.
You realise that you have run your first four minute mile.
You do two hundred press ups before your morning meal
What a sense of well being the wee pill makes you feel.

Before the pills are finished you're feeling oh so grand,
Surely Dr. Jordan is the best in all the land.
You run the errands, do the chores and don't get out of puff,
No matter what you seem to do you haven't done enough.

What you do not realise, the point that you have missed,
The doctor also happens to be a good psychologist.
It wasn't the pills that she prescribed that made you feel this way,
But the little conversation, before going on your way.

When you go to the surgery, it shouldn't be a shock,
If you don't get medication but instead a little talk.
She knows that what you tell her can remove that mental block,
Just remember that placebo' and ask her…
"What's Up Doc?"

A BOTANICAL WONDERLAND

There is lily of the valley
And forget-me-nots to see.
There are daffodils by Wordsworth
And orchids for brides to be.
Lobelias, dahlias, tulips
And gladioli on the ground.
Carnations always seem to spread their beauty all around.
Children making daisy chains
It fills your heart with glee,
Petunias, violets, buttercups
What a sight to see.
The crocus shows it's lovely head
Even as the cold wind blows,
But the one which means the world to me
Is a beautiful lustrous rose.
Love was more than a word to me
It became a way of life
Upon the day' my dearest Rose
That you became my wife.
In every year that's passed since then
You've blossomed' bloomed and grew,
Your love and strength and fortitude
Have always seen us through.
The six small seedlings that we bred
Are growing day by day
Susan, Edward, Margaret
Maturing in every way.
Matthew, Marc and Katie
Have still to bloom and shine
But with patience, love and tender care
They will to the end of time.
There are three other flowers growing
And in a not too distant day
They'll have the joy of their offspring
For such is nature's way.

TO MY SON

I love you more than the sun that glows
And even more than the wind that blows
And more so, even, than the moon that shines
Or snow that falls in flakes so fine
For when you glow just like the sun
You brighten up my life, my son.

For when your happy, I'll recall
The times that matter most of all
Is the happiness you brought to me
And opened my eyes to let me see
When it fills my heart, to overflow
The love, that you, to me do show
And when you walk, or when you run
You walk with me, for you're my son.

When you cry it makes me sad
And think of good times that we've had
When the rain it drops, in rivulets
Until the soil around it wets
And the child who plays within the park
Or the light that lightens up the dark
For through the years I've watched you grow
So that your innermost thoughts I know
And when the day is almost done
You know I love you, for you're my son.

Sometimes we talk of things you do
Your mum and I , and the other kids too
We talk of things that you would say
Of you getting on in your own quiet way
When you laugh we laugh with you
And when you cry then we cry too
So when these things are said and done
They're said with you in mind, my son.

And when your mum and I do walk
At the end of life's long weary road
You'll speak of us in happy talk
And help to lighten , others' load.
These things I wish and hope are done
I know they will , for you're my son.

TAKE A BUTCHER'S AT THIS

If you've come to the shopping centre to spend your hard earned pay
Then stop at Lawrence the Butcher, It'll really make your day
Big Bill is at the counter giving his usual spiel
"If you buy twenty three, get another one free, now that's a brilliant deal!
Would you like a pound of mince hen, or a pound and a half of stew?
Or a lovely bit of sirloin steak, from an Aberdeen Angus coo?
Spare ribs, ham haugh, black pudding, or a couple of nice pigs feet?
With a plate of totties and cabbage, It'll go right down a treat"

Wee john steps in for a customer, "perhaps you'd like to try
A beautiful steak and kidney, mince round or killie pie?
There's raw beef ham or bacon, (shepherd's pie is yours to bake)
And if you're feeling religious, try a bit of popeseye steak.
There's corned beef or gammon, and I know you wouldn't gripe
If tomorrow night you came home to a lovely pot of tripe.

And I wouldn't like to put you into a financial hole
So here's two pounds of stewing steak for the perfect casserole.
There's coo's for beef, and pig's for pork, there's even ewe or ram
Could you think of anything nicer, than a lovely leg of lamb?
There isn't any venison, and there's a simple reason
They've even shut the stag's head pub, (the beast is out of season).
It's customer care we think of when you step inside the door
We'll offer any meat you like, you couldn't ask for more

So when you read this poem, come in, we'd like to meet
A customer, just like yourself, so give yourself a treat
We're a personal shop, we aren't like the giant superstore
If you come in now, you'll come again, and come again some more
Step in and spend a few bob, for there is nothing worse
Than sitting at home with no meat, and money in your purse.

THE GREATEST

There is a man, who is the greatest man you'll ever see
Greater than louis, Marciano, or even Muhammad Ali.
On the football field he was better than Slim Jim, or Georgie Best,
Wee Jimmy J, or the great Pele, would have to take a rest.
As an actor, he outclassed Cagney, and where Bogart got his line
"Of all the bars in all the world, you ended up in mine"
When he sang, Sinatra listened, Pavarotti stood amazed
Perry Como hung his head in shame, Domingo just felt dazed.
When he ran in the mile, he stopped for a while, half way round to have a pee
He was pipped at the post by a second at most, by a man called Roger B.
In the Falklands war he took Tumbledown Ridge, he was just a fighting machine
So they later sent him to the Persian Gulf, to sort out Saddam Hussein.
He built the San Francisco Bridge, working from an old shipwreck
And rebuilt the Statue Of Liberty, during his dinner break.
He was once an Astronaut you know, but only for a little while
He was also a Sculptor, and that's why the man in the moon has a permanent smile.
When he played golf he was an Ornithologist, and the reason is plain to see
Eagles and Birdies at every hole, with amazing regularity.
I stand by every word I've said, without fear of defamation
Not one single line contains the slightest exaggeration.
I could swear on a stack of bibles, without fear or temerity
For the guy that I am writing about…
Just happens to be me.

MURPHY'S LAW

You step into the taxi which is 20 minutes late
The driver is a grouch behind the wheel
There is no conversation till you reach your destination
And you can't explain how angry that you feel.

He has charged you £12.50 for a fifteen minute drive
But you only have a ten and five pound note
He hasn't any change, and your just glad to be alive
For 22 and a half (%) he's got your goat.

So you go into the restaurant to enjoy your evening meal
You have been told, this is the place to be
But the table that you booked, has been somehow overlooked
So you'll have to give a bung to the Maitre'D.

When you sit down at the table in the corner of the room
And Manuel the waiter serves you with your meal
The soup is cold. The wine is hot, and finally so are you
For he serves you up with Ham instead of Veal.

Now you're at the Royal Concert Hall and you are not amused
Due to problems unforeseen the show is dead
Dr Hook cannot appear ' cause the drug test wasn't clear;
They're appearing at the Sheriff Court instead.

So your whole night out's been ruined from the start up to the end
Nothing else can go wrong, so you would have thought
But Murphy's law has started, so you haven't got a friend
And it's time to understand that that's your lot.

Now you're in the Hospital, you've been rushed to A and E
Food poisoning is the Doctor's diagnosis
And you know that he's correct, there is nothing circumspect
If you believe in Murphy's Law, that's the prognosis.

Now you know that lousy meal with the Ham instead of Veal
Gave you Botulism poisoning, that is why
Salmonella won the fight, and although it isn't right
You now have a serious case of E-Coli.

There is no point in bleating, that the meal you had been eating
Had contaminated Ham or the Coleslaw
And though the feeling's fleeting, that your God you may be meeting
You know it was caused because of Murphy's Law.

'KATIE' (AGED 3)

"Good Morning Mum, Good Morning Dad", I can hear her say…
but I can only think what kind of start to any day
so she'll climb onto our bed now, and bounce, my how she'll bounce
I think that she must weigh about ten stones if she's an ounce
It's now just turned 6.30 and the sun has lit the dark
But Katie has no sense of time, she rises with the Lark
She thinks today is just today, tomorrow's out of sight
But Katie being Katie thinks that everything's alright
So now she's brought her toy's in, just so she can play
She's like a ray of sunshine that brightens up the day
And now she's woken Marcus up, so he can join in
It's bad enough with one, with two, it's just a constant din
Now Katie's having breakfast, it'll be Cornflakes as well
Katie loves her Cornflakes, she thinks they're really swell
Then it's time to get her face washed, and then to comb her hair
But when you turn round to get Katie, she's no longer there
It's time to go to Playschool now, her mind is in a whirl
She loves the fun she has there, for she's a Playschool girl
Katie in the afternoon, would bring you to the ground
For everywhere that Katie goes, she always runs around
Katie's down to sleep now, after a tiring day of play
But I know what will happen at the dawn of the new day
"Good Morning Mum, Good Morning Dad", I can hear her say…

IT'S A DOGS LIFE

You can have a Pyrenean Mountain Dog or even a Saint Bernard
A Daschund, Corgi, or Basset Hound, Alsatians would be on guard
French Poodles are quite beautiful, in an ornamental sense
For safety I'd use a Doberman inside the perimeter fence.

We know for hunting rabbit's, Jack Russell's are the tool
But if we hunt for bigger game the Lurcher is no fool
Rottweiller's need a muzzle, to keep them safe and yet
Staffordshire's are not the sort to be kept as a pet.

Retrievers are still used to track, and trail or hunt the foe
Pointers are still used to find, wild duck or even doe
We have the wee Chihuahua breed of Mexican descent
That can't come close to the Bloodhound, for picking up the scent/

Red Setters add some colour to the canine hunting breed
And Pekingese add oriental flavour on a lead
The Boxer has the kind of face to scare you dead with fright
But the little Skye Terrier, won't give up without a fight

If I fancy a game of dominoes, Dalmatians I will play
If you want to cross the snow and ice then Huskies will do today
The Labrador guides sightless people safely down the street
But we know the Greyhound dog will surely drag you off your feet

For guarding sheep, the Border Collie surely gives his all
And the King Charles Spaniel, accompanies you, on the way to the Huntsman's Ball
But mongrel dogs can give you so much love and so much joy
Whether it be a little bitch, or even a little boy

But the one which matters most to me, is the leader of the pack
We rely on her , she relies on us, and she answers to the name of ...
ZAK.

AN ODE TO MY SON (JOHNNIE)

On the tenth day of January
In the year of ninety seven
After the pain of childbirth
I was in seventh heaven
For after nine months waiting
Came a pure unbridled joy
When the midwife turned to me and said
"Annemarie, you have a boy!"

as I held him to my bosom
contemplating this little lad
I knew my life had meaning then
I'd never felt so glad
So I thank God
For the little bundle of pure energy
And I'll give my life to bringing up
My darling son , Johnnie.

My parents are really overjoyed
Looking after my little one
And I'm so proud to have given them
A beautiful grandson
Now the first year of his life is o'er
With the next one still to come
And together we will step into the new millennium.

Then through his years of growing up
He'll know that I am there
To love him and to hold him
And show how much I care
And when I'm in my twilight years
At the setting of the sun
He'll know how much he means to me
My lovely first born son.

To Johnnie
With love
From Mum

S.O.S.

As I sit in the alcohol unit
With thoughts drifting all through my mind
Like where should I be, or who could I see
Or would we share a bottle of wine.

See I know there's a demon inside of me
In my mind , or my soul or my heart
But if I'm really going to beat the devil
Then he and I's company must part.

For I look at the people around me
Big Tam and wee Dickie and Cairns
I'm luckier than them, for I can go home
To a life with my wife and my bairns.

You see, we have all been there before
On a sea of alcohol, just afloat
The problem I find, for life's so unkind
There's a bloody great hole in the boat

We have tried to repair this problem before
But I find that we're just sinking fast
For you can't mend an alcohol hole in a ship
With a wee strip of Elastoplast.

So now we're in dry dock, repair crew are working
They're trying to get us back to sea
Not the alcohol ocean, to which we have been
But one filled with best Tetley Tea.

Now every crew member, must try to remember
At action stations to be nowhere else
Lest we run aground, or the ship's going down
Then it's every bloody man for himself

For the alcohol ocean has millions of wrecks
Littered around it's sea floor
And if this lot won't learn to keep swabbing the decks
Then I ain't going back anymore...

SMACK ON

**Down to the depths of darkness
Through the gates of hell
Into the eye of the tiger
One can never tell
If you chase the dragon
You'll find out in time
That when the dragon chases you
It's really for your mind
For very soon he'll own you
Body, soul and heart
And you will do most anything
To keep these things apart
You'll beg and steal and borrow
To keep that world at bay
And tell yourself time and again
It's only for today
Tomorrow
You'll beat the devil
And you'll believe that's it
But tomorrow never comes
It's time for another hit
It's easier to walk through the eye of a needle
Than to leave that needle alone
But with the help of those you love
You know it can be done
The first time that you bought a bag
Was only a year ago
Or was it 2,
Or was it 3?
I guess you'll never know**

You'll get the kids washed and dressed
But just don't have the time
The drugs come first
The kids can wait
Thing's will turn out fine
I'll go down to my mum's house
And ask her to babysit
It'll only be for an hour or two
(my god I need a hit)
how long have I been in these cells?
I nearly made the sale
Instead of that
I find that
I'm locked up in this jail
I've had three month's to ponder
And try to put thing's right
I know at the end of every tunnel
There always is a light
Every cloud has a silver lining
And mine is shining bright
And with god's help
I'll go through
A carefree
Drug free night

P.S. For ever.

PUT IT IN WRITING

Out of sight is out of mind, at least that's what they say,
But absence makes the heart grow fonder, with every passing day,
A friend in need, is a friend indeed, so we all need someone,
And as surely as the sun will rise, it goes down when the day is done.

If we could see what lies ahead, we'd look before we leap,
If life was really sacred, then it wouldn't come so cheap,
Everything that goes up, eventually comes down,
In fact what we are saying is, what goes round comes around.

Time or tide waits for no man, when we're late, that's what we find,
When we rely on someone, we're out of sight and out of mind,
The salt of the earth is someone, on whom we can rely,
And seeing is believing, but we all turn a blind eye.

We always hurt the one's we love, but it shouldn't be that way,
If we stopped to think, then we would try to live life for today,
Beauty is in the beholder's eye and what we sow we reap,
The first cut is the deepest, and beauty is skin deep.

Red sky at night is the shepherd's delight and the early bird gets the worm,
And birds of a feather flock together, like the calm before the storm,
A watched kettle never boils, we say that time stands still,
I'll love you till forever, or that is until...

We cut the ties that bind us, but you can't keep a good man down,
And laughter we're told, is good for the soul, till we cry the tears of a clown,
We hear of ships that pass in the night, or any port in a storm,
A vision of loveliness to me, is the rainbows lovely form.

And yet, when all is said and done, the moral still rings true,
Sticks and stones may break your bones, but names just can't hurt you,
If music be the food of love, and we live by the written word,
Then the truest saying must be, (The pen is mightier than the sword).

You've made you're bed, so lie in it, or just get on your bike,
The bigger the fool, the harder the fall, and you can take a hike,
A fool and his money are easy to part, but you can't get blood from a stone,
We want to be far from the madding crowd, but we don't want to be alone.

Some people can be seen but not heard, or cause trouble in an empty house,
Some like empty vessels make the most noise, and some are quiet as a mouse,
If the going up, should get you down, or if shove should come to push,
Always remember a bird in the hand, is worth two in the bush.

Every cloud has a silver lining, from the dark there comes a light,
Always stand by your principles, don't go down without a fight,
Remember these old sayings, or even the odd adage,
And maybe soon we'll add them to the bottom of this page.

PEOPLE

**When you're going about your business, or just walking down the street,
A friend that you are passing, or a neighbour that you meet,
That just to stop to say hello, can really make their day,
And help those people look at life in a totally different way.**

**For people like to know that, other people care,
About the thing's that they do, or even the clothes they wear,
For people are much happier, if people stop to say,
"How are thing's going", "mind yourself" or "have a lovely day"
We know some people go through life, hardly saying a word,
Of kindness, to other people, now isn't that absurd,
If people asked, how are the kids, or how's your mum and dad,
And showed a little concern for them, they wouldn't be so sad.**

**Then they in turn would do the same the next time that they meet
So when they go on their way, they'd be more light upon their feet
And when they pass that feeling, onto the next in line
Then people all begin to feel the world is going fine
Because people need each other, to go another mile
It would be a whole lot easier to do it with a smile
And make our earthly journey seem a little more worthwhile
If you stop and take the time of day, you're doing it in style.**

**But people, being people, just can't be all the same
Otherwise we'd be as well, using the same name
But if we raised our hand in friendship, our neighbours to extend
Then we wouldn't be just people, but really, truly, friends.**

IT'S A ROSE

**There is a beautiful flower, which all year round's in bloom
You can feel it's radiance, when you walk into the room
For when you're in it's presence, it can make you feel
Dizzy, with it's strength and grace, it makes the senses reel.**

**It's been there, for many years, for one score years or so
And yet it never withers, it's age will never show
It has always blossomed there, through rain and snow, and shine
And I believe it always will, until the end of time.**

**For I, have always heard it said, that love can never die
And love's a feeling from the heart, that never questions why
Although the stalk may weaken, like satin the petals stay
In my mind's eye, I do perceive, a beautiful bouquet.**

**And when it's gently handled, your skin it can't be torn
For this is one fine flower, that doesn't have a thorn
It's leaves protect it's seedlings, which all around it grows
You know, this lovely flower's my wife, my pretty darling Rose.**

THE MAN IN THE MOON

**Last night I was watching the man in the moon
And a smile on his face I could see
It may sound absurd, but when I heard these words
I knew he was speaking to me.**

**"For millions of years, through man's trials and fears
I've watched them with my happy face
I don't know why
But I've seen them all try
To destroy the whole human race**

**First with clubs and stone axes, then arrows and spears
Then bullets and bombs finally
I've watched humans trying, through anger and tears
Try to blow earth to infinity"**

**Then I heard myself answer the man in the moon
"As you know man has conquered space flight
And you know it's true, since they've landed on you
It's up there that they'll carry on the fight"**

**I thought then I'd beaten the man in the moon
For the next time I looked he was gone
Then I realised, though not really surprised
He had just disappeared with the dawn.**

**Tonight I won't look at the man in the moon
And there's no doubt that he will be there
For the night that he's not, then there won't be a jot
Of humanity left anywhere.**

**So let us all pray that the Lord cares as much
For the moon as he does for the earth
In creating the heavens, he was quite right
For mankind can now prove it's worth.**

TO A ROBIN

If I could fly like an eagle, to the heavens I would soar
Or like an albatross, I would sail on, forever more
If I was travelling anywhere, I'd be a swift, for speed
Spanning distance very quickly, would be very fine indeed

For showing off real beauty, then a peacock I would be
And when I showed my plumage, then what a sight you'd see
To never feel pangs of hunger, I'd be a starling on the ground
Starlings always seem to find, any scraps that are around

Or if I felt that sometimes I would like a tasty dish
Then just like an osprey I would angle for some fish
If I wanted to be an ostrich, then I could have great fun
Me and other ostriches, going for a run

For holding conversations I would be a mynah bird
Everybody else would be stuck for bloomin' words
So then I'd be a parrot, and I'd repeat, and then repeat
Monologues, or poetry, or music by the sheet

To be extremely elegant, I'd have to be a swan
And anywhere that I would go, a floor show I'd put on
I'd hate to be a vulture, it must be pure strife
Waiting for the casualties of other wild life

Or I could be a humming bird and hover o'er the ground
My heart and wings beating fast, to make that humming sound
But if ever there was a bird that I'd long to be
It would be a robin redbreast, and the reason is you see

That every year at Christmas I'd fill children's hearts with glee
For they'd see me on their Christmas cards, and wish that they were me.

ANOTHER FISHY TAIL

At the very top of the aquatic scale, he's known as Orca, the killer whale.
And down below, on the fishing line, you'll take the sea trout from Loch Fyne.
Delphinus Delphus makes his mark, he's ten times smarter than the great white shark.
The king on the river has got to be the Salmon, on his way to the sea.
For tuna and marlin we cross the pond, with the fishing fraternity,
There is a bond.
For everyday eating there is cod and skate
And mackerel and herring to put on your plate
There's scampi, squid and octopus
They gorge themselves till they're fit to bust
And if your fishing for a couple of ray, or flounders or plaice, then the place is the bay
If you want to try fishing without rod or reel
Then you should try lobster, you just need a creel
If you don't want to run into Moby the whale
Then maybe you should settle for a nice prawn cocktail
There's catfish and dogfish, lesser spotted, and yet,
They aren't the sort you could keep as a pet
During the war, subs used iron fish
They called them torpedoes, more like scuttlefish
With pilchards and sardines jammed in their tin
You eat every morsel from nose to tail fin
There are thousands of species of fish 'neath the waves
On coral, in shipwrecks, and undersea caves
They can brighten or frighten or bring harmony
To other poor Sole who inhabit the sea
On the arctic ice floes you will find playful seals
Till the polar bear strikes, then you'll hear their squeals
'tween the swordfish and hammerhead shark there's no choice
I think I'd prefer just a gentle porpoise
Why starfish are so named, yet live in the sea
And fish made of jelly, but not by Rowntree
Whelks, mussels and cockles, oysters and clams
And conch shells that weigh maybe 5 kilograms
Barracuda, I don't like, cause he's hard and lean
And he lives his life as a killing machine
The only sea I know where there aren't any fish
Is the sea of tranquillity, and the reason is this
To get there you wouldn't be going to Neptune
But our other satellite, which is known as the moon

So I've weighed up the pros and cons of it all
There's only one fish which is good for the soul
Costs buttons to feed, and just 3 inches small
My pet goldfish jaws, at play in his bowl
Now Darwin, he helped us to realise the scale
Of the difference, from anemone to the whale
And with television, a hero came through
To educate us all, and his name, Jacques Cousteau
That's why France is noted by Egon Ronay
You can wash down your caviar with a wee Beaujolais
But I draw the line when it comes to frog's legs
I'd tell them to hop it and just keep their eggs
With Pisces, my star sign, an angler I'll be
Living life from Earths larder, the great deep blue sea
Jesus fed the multitude with loaves and fishes, ten
And said he wanted us to be, his Fishers of men
So I'll finish as I started, with another fishy tale
The hero of the story
Not Jonah, but the whale.

YOU DIRTY RAT

A mechanic's a technician, who takes a car apart
From top to bottom and back to front, until it breaks his heart
This happened because the owner, heard a little tiny squeak
For the car he bought, was meant to be, made of pure oak, not teak

The car's in a thousand pieces, all scattered on the floor
The technician's now a mechanic on his way out of the door
Cause it wasn't the carburettor, or differential
Accelerator, brakes, or clutch or gears, or corrosion on the sills

After he left, the boy came by, and heard another squeak
So he decided with nothing to do, that he would have a peek
When he saw the little thing, between the car exhaust
He wondered why, the garage, had gone to such a cost

Surely a forty thousand pound shogun, four wheel drive
Was worth more than the life of, a gerbil, when alive

And when he had a feeling, of, abhorrent, utmost dread
He had the spanner in his hand, and the desert rat lay dead

So let this be a lesson, to every one of you
As it is to the technician, signing on at Anniesland broo
For the moral of the story, and one I know is true
If you hear a squeak, then pass the job, to the mechanic next to you.

ONE DAY IN PARADISE

**You know I've often wondered, why The Lord's day's on a Sunday
You'd think that would be the one day, they set aside as funday
The people who graft all week, working fingers to the bone
Are expected to wash the dishes, the minute they get home.**

**Why not make the Monday the day of rest instead
Geldof hated Mondays, thought, we'd all be better dead
Tuesdays should be, the starting day, that we all seek
For one way or another, it would be a shorter working week.**

**Then we could make the Monday, the Sabbath Day of rest
Having a long lie on Monday morning, would definitely be best
And if you were in employment, then wouldn't it be fine
To know that working Mondays, got you paid at double time.**

**If Tuesday through to Friday, our working week would be
We'd have a happier working class, and more relaxed, you'd see
The only problem is they'd have to raise the hourly rate
Instead of a miserable £4, they'd have to make it £8.**

**With the shorter week we'd find that, everyone could have a job
And people would be better off, we'd all have a few bob
And with all the extra money, that we'd all have to spend
Our children to Universities, we could afford to send.**

**And then with all the learning, this would be a smarter place
And we would be the leading light, of the human race
Because our brains were clearer, we would use them more
We could all sit down and talk, and put an end to war.**

**With all the money that was saved on arms expenditure
There'd be no third world countries, of that we could be sure
With an end to plague and pestilence, we'd surely realize
Our rightful place upon this earth, is really, paradise.**

ON CALL

Could you ask Doctor Robertson, to come round here real quick
My man was at the pub last night and now he's feeling sick
Dr Robertson, Dr Robertson, I know you have the gift
To prescribe a medication, to give my man a lift
I have to get him out to work so I can get my pay
If you do that Dr Robertson, it'll really make my day

Dr Robertson, Dr Robertson, the wean's no feeling well
I think it's German Measles, but only you can tell
Cause I don't speak the language (and that's not just a pun)
I only speak good English, not the language of the Hun
If any pregnant women were in your surgery
And I brought him in, he could shorten, their life's expectancy

Dr Robertson, Dr Robertson if you could take the time
To come and give my son here, a six week sickness line
For he has terrible acne, and his nose is running too
Dr Robertson, Dr Robertson, I don't know what to do
He's been watching television, from dusk till the sunrise
It's starting to affect him, cause he's got skelly eyes

Dr Robertson, Dr Robertson, I've heard that you're not well
They say that you are tired out, but only time will tell
I would come round to visit, but I just don't have the time
Just take a paracetamol and you will be just fine
I've got a tiny headache now, so I hope that you will come
But if you cannot manage, would you send round your Locum.

JESUS WAS A CARPENTER

Jesus was a Carpenter, two thousand years ago
Who died on a cross in Calvary, aged thirty years or so
On the eve of his death, in Gethsemane he had spent the night
Speaking to his father , in Heaven above, hoping to ease his plight
"Let this cup, pass to someone else", but it could not be done
For though it broke his fathers heart, he gave his only begotten son
To crowning with thorns, and scourging, and crucifixion too
Saying, "Father, forgive them, for they know not what they do"
Before his death, he had told the scribes, he would rise on the third day
They laughed, and jeered, and scoffed at him, till the stone was rolled away
The Apostles began to spread the word, to those who came to hear
That Jesus died upon the cross, the sins of man to clear
Now Matthew, Mark, and Luke and John, travelled near and far
And told the story of the child, born under the Bethlehem Star
And to combat evil on this Earth, had to be justified
So God gave, his only son, Jesus, to be crucified
Later on, the Holy Bibles, words they did unfold
And opened peoples eyes to, the greatest story ever told
Now we're older and much wiser, or so we'd have it thought
That for thirty pieces of Silver, we surely can't be bought
But we walk upon this earth now, Masters of all we survey
Forgetting the price, the Good Lord paid, on the Cross on Calvary
So if we loved our neighbours, as ourselves, wouldn't it be great
Knowing that the world was meant, for love, instead of hate
And children could all grow up, as friend instead of foe
Singing " Onward Christian Soldiers" as through their lives they go
So that when they finally reach out, to meet their final goal
Jesus Christ will take to him, each and every soul
And keep them for Eternity, in never ending love
With himself and all his Angels in his mansions up above.

HEY BABY I'M THE TELEPHONE MAN

With a name like Angela, she must have a face to match
When the telephone rings, she dons her wings, and plays upon her harp
For the guys who call must know that, when they pay their L.S.D.
By the time the call is over, they will be in ecstacy.

For Angela has a telephone voice, with a really sexy sound
The sort of voice which picks you up, when you are feeling down
I wish I knew her number, I would phone her every night
To cheer me up and make me feel, the world was bang to rights
I know I'd be much happier, well, that is until
British Telecom, sent me a whopping great big bill.

So if you don't give me her number, it will be one saving grace
To have a few quid in the bank, but no smile upon my face
Angie will be happy with the money that she saves
But spare a thought for all the guys who'll rest in paupers graves.

As a neighbour I'm glad you have her, to talk to, and extend
A shoulder for you to cry on, and show you she's your friend
For we all need somebody, on whom we can depend
So that when the shoe's on the other foot, your shoulder you will lend.

If I've told you once, I've told you twice, but now, let me remind
That a friend in need, is a friend indeed, and very hard to find
As we go down life's highway, it can be a lonely walk
But as Bob Hoskins tells us on TV., you know, "it's good to talk."

A VERY SPECIAL FRIEND

To get to where you are now, took a dozen years, and more
But now that you have gotten there, you're knocking on heaven's door
So all the tears and hard work, haven't been in vain
Because, now that you have reached your goal, it's laughter instead of pain.

We know how hard it must have been, on those steps along the way
But the 17th of April '96, was your really special day
You know that George and Jonathon, must be really filled with pride
Knowing that they were with you, standing side by side..

Your other son Chris, your mother, and your brothers and sisters too
And friends and acquaintances, know no one, deserves it more than you
You have been a perfect mother and an excellent wife as well
And a very good daughter and sister, of that we all can tell.

Marina, you have always been, a special friend to me
Always there in my times of need, and helped to make me see
That even when things look dark, there always is a light
With a bit of love and patience, things will turn out right.

To get the job you wanted, and diplomas, I knew you should
Because no one deserved them more, that's why I knew you would
And please remember one thing, until our journey's end
You'll always and forever, be, my very special friend.

From Rosemary

VIVA ESPANA

Wee Suzie's won a holiday, she's struck lucky once again
So now herself and Wattie are jetting off to Spain
They'll spend a fortnight bathing in the Costa Del Sol Sun
Drinking Pina Coladas 'til the day is almost done.

With a couple of joints to help them, going up and coming down
And the Spanish sunshine turning them, a lovely shade of brown
Suzie was going to take her toy boy with her, going abroad
But Walter said if that was the case, then she'd go on her todd.

So Wattie's going to have a shave, to lose ten years or more
So that he can be her toy boy, sitting on that Spanish shore
Walter will take with him, an extra few quid, there's no doubt
So that they can bring back, a massive carry out.

24 bottles of whisky and the same of Smirnoff
when he gets back to Yoker, he will be like Joe the Toff
and in the depths of winter, they'll look back and they'll say
"wasn't that great, we just had, our Spanish holiday!"

DREAMLAND

I heard of a land where there is no greed
Where those who have, give to those in need
There is a land that is full of love
Where all believe in God above
I saw a land that had no dead
Where no one hurt, and no one bled
I walked a land of milk and cream
Then I awoke, twas just a dream.

A TRIBUTE TO KRIS KRISTOFFERSON

I've listened to Willie Nelson
And Johnny Cash is something great
Hank Williams was really special
Until he met his fate
but it wasn't until the70s, that you sang a song for me
it was also for, everybody else
but it was Me And Bobby McGee
Billy Dee was 17 when he turned 21
John Garfield's Blues, were for John Prine
For he's the 2nd son
Lovin Her Was Easier, the second time around
But I hate to think of me going through
Sunday Morning, Coming Down
Jesus Was A Capricorn, and maybe he was right
But I guess I'll never really know
I'M Out Of Mind, And Out Of Sight
There's an Okie From Muskogee
Who, For The Good Times, he knew
Rainbow Road and The Pilgrim and The Epitaph (Black And Blue)
Jesse Younger, was the type of man that I might have become
But then I listened to Breakdown, (A Long Long Way From Home)
I think that Beat The Devil, was the best you ever did
But I also loved, The Taker, and Jody And The Kid
I hope that I can listen to you until the day I die
From The Other Side Of Nowhere, to The Silver Tongued Devil And I
I'm glad you Beat the Devil, cause you know, Nobody Wins
As all through Darby's Castle, we all answer for our sins
In the 20 odd years I've heard you, I knew that it was right
Cause just like Gladys, you Help Me To Make It Through The Night
I'm glad you came to Scotland, you've made my dream come true
Because of all the country greats there's been
The best of them, is you.

REMEMBER ME

**If I'm to be remembered, after I am gone
Then make it not for what has been
But more for what I've done
The things I said I'd like to do, should never be forgot
And all the things I didn't do, should matter not a jot.**

**The things I've done throughout my life
Whether they be bad or good
If benefit to someone else, then be that as it should
With people, all throughout my life, I tried to do what's right
And if things didn't go as planned, I always hoped they might.**

**The friends and neighbours I have known, all mattered much to me
Remember there are none so blind, as he who will not see
The relatives and family, that I love so much
Through the good and through the bad and even out of touch
The wife and children that are mine, made my life seem so bright
We tried to bring the kids up, to know what's wrong from right.**

**When the quality of life to me seemed to lose it's zest
I only know I really tried, to always do my best
So if you do remember me, then know I'd always try
And think "but for the grace of God, there go you or I"
Think of things all said and done, in work and rest and play
And for the good, and for the bad, remember me, this way.**

A WINTER WONDERLAND

**When snow starts falling, in flakes so fine
Then children shout "its wintertime
We'll build a snowman, and have a snowball fight
Then we'll make a slide, and we'll sledge till night"
And when they come home, all cold and blue
Then mum will make them a nice hot brew
She'll put on their PJs and tuck them in bed
And read them a story, Snow White and Rose Red
When the children are sleeping, their dreams will be full
Of Santa and Rudolph and everything Yule
And when they awaken and look out to see
Their snowman still standing, they'll be filled with glee
While adults all think this weather's a crime
To children, the best season is, wintertime.**

ALICE

A, is for all the years that you spent with me
L, is for the love we'll share, for all eternity
I, is for infinity, I know it means the same
C, is for the children, that each we gave a name
E, is for every day we've spent throughout the years

L, is for the life we've spent, in laughter and in tears
E, is for the everything's, that you share with me
E, is for each other, that's how it will always be

You know I love you Alice and I know that you'll get well
For, what's around the corner, no one can ever tell
We've had our ups and had our downs, and always seen them through
From the bottom of my heart dear, you know, that I love you.

Fae your other hauf
Big Jai.

IN THE DOGHOUSE

Hello, my name is Brambles, and I am glad that's so
If I'd been bought at Christmas, I could have been mistletoe
Instead of scrabbling through my life, a lucky dog I'll be
For my mistress is a Doctor, I'm an honorary G.P.

Although I'm fostered out now, I have to paws, for thought
Robertsons Jam and Brambles, go together quite a lot
She takes me out for walkies, though runnings not the same
A bit of exercise will help, and I will take the blame.

I know I'm therapeutic and the reasons plain to see
Apart from being mans best friend, I like female company
I know we have to be apart so you can do what's right
Otherwise I wouldn't have given you up without a fight.

I know it's just a dogs life, so my senses I will hone
And I'll con Dr. Robertson for an extra doggie bone
She's a good foster mistress, and tries to do what's right
But as a canine, I should know, she lacks that extra bite.

I'm dropping you this poem, to let you know I am
Your caring, loving "Brambles" and not a pot of jam
Absence makes the heart grow fonder, well that's what they say
So I'll just bide my time and love you more and more each day.

You know I don't like pussycats, us canines know its right
Although I wouldn't hurt one, my barks worse than my bite
I'll be glad when you come home, and maybe then you'll see
The owner and the dog are just perfect company.

McNAIR HOUSE (GARTNAVEL)

**In the grounds of Gartnavel, at the edge of the perimeter
There's a place for folk with problems, it's known as the House McNair
If your problems are mental, drugs or alcohol
And your at the end of your tether, it will be your port of call.**

**For the staff there, all understand the problems people face
And try to get the patients back among the human race
It isn't easy working, with one's who are so fragile
But with quite a good success rate, it makes it all worthwhile**

**You are treated there with dignity, and the utmost charm
And made to feel that in their care, you will not come to any harm
I was there in '94 and made substantial gain
But if at first you don't succeed, try, try, and try again.**

**If I can make it this time, then it will change my life
Not only to myself but to my children and my wife
And if a zest for living, in me it can arouse
Then thankful I will always be, to the place called McNair House.**

**I think that Dr. Kershaw started out this whole idea
And if so, then he did fine, in his chosen career
His unfinished work has now been left in the hands of his protégé
And Dr. Smith has got it right, for what will be, will be.**

**There are thousands of other patients, who'll agree with what I say
Just try to live life to the full, by living day to day
Vince and Dom and Michael, and the rest of the McNair team
Are getting there in every way, fulfilling their working dream.**

**I hope they go on to better things, in all they try to do
From the bottom of my heart, I say, good luck, and God bless you.**

THE HIGHWAY TO HEAVEN

**As you go along life's highway, do you ever wonder why
From the moment that you are born, you then, begin to die
And everything that's in between is just a fact of life
That some days, that we go through, are like the sharp side of a knife
And other days it seems like everything's going really well
But what's around the corner, no one can ever tell
No person should ever know, what lies ahead of them
Whether its as dull, as dull can be, or sparkle like a gem
When you go down life's happy road, or lonely avenue
You'll meet others who're going through, the same things that you do
And if you're lucky then you'll meet, that very special one
Who wants to spend their life with you, till the setting of the sun
You'll meet many people, different in every way
It's up to you to understand, the things they do and say
You'll care for some, then find that, life can be unjust
There'll be those, who let you down, the one's you shouldn't trust
And there'll be one's that you'll be proud, to look upon as friend
The one's who'll go through thick and thin, until the journey's end
And when you're in your twilight years, among those whom you love
You can look back through the years, and give thanks to God above
For giving you the chance to meet, the people you did meet
From the very beginning, to the end of life's main street
And when up to the junction, of the end of life's long drive
You know, it was you, who made the choices, when alive
That determine whether you go left, or whether you go right
And hopefully that when you turn, you'll see a shining light
And in that instant, you will know, you're going through a special door
To spend your new life with your God, for now and ever more**

IN A CLASS OF THEIR OWN

On the 13th of March 1996, the world began to weep
For it was the day we realised that even God may sleep
Sixteen lovely children became Angels on that day
And their teacher, Gwen, went with them, to help to pave the way
When Gwen awakened Jesus, to put them in his care
Jesus said, they were the nicest Angels, anywhere
We know the families suffered, in every single case
I only hope they realise that Heaven's a happier place
For Jesus only borrowed off, he gave them out on loan
The way they are, is the way they were, in a class of their own
Being Cherubim and Seraphim to Jesus Christ on high
Watching o'er their loved ones, till their Earthly time goes by
Until all are joined together on the Final Judgement Day
To hear the King of Kings proclaim for all eternity
"Suffer the little children who did come unto me
To be with all the Angels and Saints, and Holy Trinity"
Now if everyone would recite the Lord's Prayer line for line
We'd surely come to realise, it is really quite sublime
The depth and meaning in the words help us understand
That being good faithful Christians
Means
We'll sit at God's right hand.

FIELDS OF LIFE

There are fields of crops the world o'er
The farmers work to tend
On which people the world over
Always can depend
The farmer ploughs and sows and works
From morning until night
Yet there are millions dying of hunger
That surely isn't right
Its politics which determine
Where all the foodstuffs go
Politicians always seem to think
Its only they who know
There are fields of dreams in every land
Where sportsmen train and play
Hoping they will represent
Their country some day
They can only give their all, blood
Sweat, and tears, until
Olympic greatness waits for them
The ultimate pinnacle
But its politics which determine
Who will go and who will stay
Its politicians who decide, who will, or will not play
There are battlefields throughout the globe
Where wars are won and lost
Where soldier fights with soldier
No matter what the cost
They may not know the reason
They have joined in the fray
To soldier, killing soldier
It is just another day

But its politics which determine
Where these killing fields lie
Politicians never have to go
To war
To live or die
But in my field of vision
I perceive in my minds eye
A world where no one hungers
And where sportsmen can but try
And its only Christian soldiers
Armed with only faith
Spreading the word of love and hope
Among the human race
there'd be no politicians, their words to bend and twist
In a world full of trust and charity, we would finally all exist.

THE LIGHT OF THE WORLD

**As the sun goes down, and I look out, on the banks of the River Clyde
And see the myriad of lights, sparkle on either side
At night the panoramic view, would take your breath away
And make you feel that, you are, only living for today.**

**Whether the tide , is in or out, you cannot really tell
But the shipyard cranes they stand out, like giant sentinels
On the tops of the multi storey flats, you can see the beacon lights
Warning, approaching aeroplanes, that they must exceed that height.**

**While the stars above they twinkle, and glisten, oh so bright
They look like a shimmering display, of heavenly Christmas lights
As the street lights all stretch away, down on the other side
After they end, you know you're at the mouth of the River Clyde.**

**All over the country, people are going from A to B
Using the artificial lights, without which they would not see
The boats going down the river, on the left or on the right
Wouldn't be able to operate, without navigation lights.**

**When the man in the moon goes back to bed, and the sun comes out to play
And there's light and brightness everywhere, to help you on your way
Without lights, we would only have twelve hours, in which to live and be
And we know that there are none so blind, as he who will not see.**

**So we'll say a prayer and thank the Lord, for giving us the light
To follow the path he gave us out of mind and out of sight
We may take his path and follow him, or we may choose to rescind
But remember life's as fragile, as a candle in the wind.**

**I hope I am there on Judgement Day, when God's greatness is unfurled
And our eyes are opened wide to see, the true light of the world.**

THE GUARDIAN ANGEL

**As a primary school teacher, her vocation it was clear
To bring the best out in the children, placed within her care
For they loved her and trusted her, she helped to make them see
That they could have their education, and like Mrs Mayor be
For Gwen was so respected, and loved by all she knew
To her home life and her working life, she was completely true
Before the thirteenth day of March, she probably didn't see
As well as being a wife and mum, a Guardian Angel she would be
The Good Lord must have chosen Gwen, for her to show the way
To the sixteen children in her care, and calm their fears that day
We know these kids are happy now, in Jesus' sweet embrace
For their teacher has now taught them, that Heaven's a better place
Because there are seventeen new stars, to brighten up the sky
And answer the question on everyone's lips, the one we all ask, "why?"
Gwen's husband Rod, will never forget, what happened that fateful day
And her children will always remember, when she was called away
For it was the day the world stood still, in anguish and in pain
And people the whole world over, turned their thoughts to the town, Dunblane
We know God moves in mysterious ways, his laws to show are true
And, but for the grace of God, there goes me or you
To combat evil on this earth, has to be justified
That's why God gave his only son, Jesus, to be crucified
And why we all should say a prayer, for peace between all men
That Gwen and her pupils, will rest in peace, now, and forever…Amen**

SUSAN

I remember well, when you were born, and I looked upon your face
Instead of calling you Susan, it should have been Amazing Grace
And even in your first year, I can still recall
You crawling, walking, talking, no problem at all
After that you took off, in leaps and then in bounds
And even with Ed and Margaret, it was like the fox and hounds
you were a lovely baby, and lovely child, and then you grew
into a lovely teenager, and even then we knew
that you would be more lovely when you passed the score
I think that you will always be lovely for ever more
Because you are our first born, there is a prejudice
For Rabbie Burns has told us, "Ae fond kiss"
I know that life isn't easy when you're growing up
But it tastes a little better drinking from the loving cup
One day, you will know that, what I say is true
For you will have kids of your own and then you will go through
The laughter, tears and happiness, and sadness and the joy
That special moment in your life
They tell you, "IT'S A BOY!"

So now that day has finally dawned, wee Stephen's on your knee
And we could say, Que c'era (or what will be, will be)
He'll bring joy and happiness, to Derek and Lorraine
He'll make it seem like sunshine, even when its pouring rain
When he's a wee bit older, his dad can take him out
To the park, or zoo, or with the ball, to have a kickabout
And spending football seasons
In the Man. United stand
And even dream of playing for them
Now wouldn't that be grand
You've made us very happy with your lovely little one
Rosemary is really tickled pink
With her beautiful grandson
I know he'll be a credit to his mum and to his dad
And when he's grown
He'll give to them another lovely lad.

ZAK

Ally and Ger they call me Zak, for short they call me Z
They like to take me out for walks, I'd rather stay in bed
They feed me beef or rabbit, but I like sirloin steak
Instead of doggie biscuits, I love Madeira cake.

They bought me cotton pyjamas, a nice wee dog to pull
I much prefer cashmere or silk, and not just cotton wool
I live the life of Reilly, I'm rarely left alone
In fact, I've just sent Gerry down, for a nice fresh doggie bone.

After I've had my dinner, I'll sleep just like a log
And then I'll go for a ten mile run, I'm fit as a butcher's dog
They'll get me dressed in my hat and scarf, and booties on my feet
With my Gucci ribbon round my neck, I'll look really neat.

They can take me down to the woolpack, or even the local pub
For an advocat aperitif, we'll go to the kennel club
I feel like the cat's whiskers, in fact my life is bliss
It's time to go to bed, so I'll have to get my goodnight kiss.

I didn't have a future
Things looked really black
'til Ally and Ger adopted me
and decided to call me Zak.

A HEAVENLY SCOTCH PIE

**When you walk into the butchers shop, it takes your breath away
To see the lovely trays of meat all laid out on display
There's sirloin steak, pork, beef and ham
Spare ribs and chops and legs of lamb
Beef links are really looking nice
And lorne, whole, or ready sliced
Black pudding side by side with white
The bacon rashers look just right
But what I'm in the shop to buy
Is my daily snack, a nice scotch pie
They don't cost much, that's why I'm sold
They're lovely hot , and lovely cold
A hot scotch pie and mushy peas, just goes down a treat
Your teeth sink through the pastry, into the beef minced meat
The hint of herbs and spices, which makes it yours to savour
A touch of vinegar and salt, to give it that special flavour
You can have it totally different, by very simple means
You can have your scotch pie topped off, with a portion of baked beans
When you eat your scotch pie in the house or at the football game
Or on a picnic with the kids, then they will want the same
The scotch pie is the perfect snack to be taken anywhere
Al Fresco or a Restaurant you'll still say that was "rerr"
It should be our other national dish, I think that would be quaint
At the end of November when we toast our Scottish Patron Saint
With a glass of scotch in one hand, in the other a braw scotch pie
And our voices in unison proclaim," Scots wha hae, och aye"
Saint Andrew could then look down and never question why
His name went hand in hand with, a freshly made scotch pie.**

THE GREAT DIVIDE

You can talk of great injustice, but you'll never turn the tide
Between rich man, poor man, beggar, there is a great divide
Prostitution, theft, or maybe drugs, I think you know the type
There's always someone smarter, who knows when the time is right
To move in, and make themselves, an extra buck or two
Won't they ever realise the cost to me and you
We try our best to make things, better than the way they were
But all we ever get to build, are castles in the air
The upper class they seem to think, to their laws, we should abide
That only they, have the given right, to have, God on their side
The rich they just get richer, and the poor, that's how they'll stay
Because Sod's Law it tells us there is no other way
But to go through life, and doff one's hat is the way its meant to be
For lords and ladies have to live, the lives of lords you see
They can spend three hundred pounds, just for one night out
For my wife and me its thirty pounds, so what's it all about?
Equality and freedom are the rights of man you see
But if some men have more power, then these things will never be
Liberty, equality, fraternity, it was once the cry
Of the people of another land, but I still do not know why
The one's who seized the power, from those who held it dear
Became the very self same one's whom the peasants feared
No man is an island, or so I've heard it said
And loneliness is not for me, far better to be dead
We have social grants, and social work, and social heights, although
We're now all anti social, so I guess we'll never know
If the one's we give a helping hand, are the one's who put us down
Until they come to realise, what goes round comes around
We know the good Lord made us in his image, plain to see
And with his grace and strength, and love, better people we would be
If we loved our neighbours, as ourselves, as the good book's read
Then there wouldn't be a great divide
But a paradise, instead.

THE MISSION

There is a place of prayer, or of meeting to one and all
To some, the Evangelical church, to others, the mission hall
To me, I know it is a place, in which to be enthralled
Because today, and every day, the good Lord's name is called.

If you start from the beginning, at the book of Genesis
And read on till the very end, you'll know that life is bliss
Life really has a meaning, on that you can depend
Because the good book tells us, from the start up to the end.

You know, the Yoker Mission Hall, has been here through the years
Alongside Yoker people, through their trials and through their tears
And through it all, it has helped, to admonish all their fears
With faith and hope , and charity, we know the good Lord hears
And if we showed charity, and hope to those we love
Then faith must be a blessing, from the good Lord up above.

We know the good Lord made us, in his image, plain to see
To glorify, and unify, and bless the Trinity
But if we do the Lord's word, we'd maybe realise
That when he died upon the cross, he left us, paradise
He didn't die for good or bad, or the colour of your face
But to ensure his lasting greatness, o'er this, our human race
And if we loved our neighbours, as ourselves, wouldn't it be great
Knowing that the world was meant, for love, instead of hate
And children could all grow up, as friends, instead of foe
Singing "Onward Christian Soldiers," as through their lives they go.

That when they finally reach out, to meet their final goal
Jesus, will take to him, each and every soul
And keep them for eternity, in never ending love
With him and all his Angels, in his mansions up above
And to think, this may all start, when you get the call
At 2420 Dumbarton Road
THE YOKER MISSION HALL.

CONSERVATION

When I look at the tree so strong and tall
Beside it, people seem so small
Through its branches children crawl
Never afraid that they might fall.

The tree has been there many years, for eighty, maybe more
The first time I looked at in awe, then, I was only four
There are thousands of children, who have climbed, through its leafy boughs
Pretending they're climbing mountains, or flying amongst the clouds.

It has always stood on guard like a giant sentinel
How deeply down its roots grow, no one can really tell
It has withstood wind and snow, and hail and heavy rain
I don't suppose I'll ever see, that great tree's like again.

They're cutting it down tomorrow, to make room for a motorway
I never once, in all my life, thought I'd ever see that day
People demonstrated, and argued it should stand
But the council *stipulated*, they needed that piece of land.

When I look at that tree so strong and tall
And know, tomorrow, it will fall
No more children through it will crawl
Now it is I, who feels so small.

GENERATIONS

When your looking for love or happiness, or not to lose, but gain
You find instead of sunshine, all that you get is rain
And as surely as the moon goes down, the sun will always rise
And this is not a hell on earth, but really paradise.

When you've met the one girl in your life, who thinks the way you do
Who knows the things you want from life, are the same things she wants too
And you're not just one person now, for you know you've won her heart
And she's sweet sixteen, and you're nineteen, but she knows you'll never part.

Now you're two years further down the road and set for married life
You asked and she accepted, so now you're man and wife
And no one else could matter so much, or so you would have thought
Till you have your kids upon your knee, their love could not be bought.

And as they grow to adulthood, you can see the patterns set
When your children each bring home to tea, the partner they have met
You can see what goes round comes around, till the circle is complete
And it won't be long till you hear the sound, of the patter of tiny feet.

Now your silver wedding has come and gone, and now you're going for gold
And your better half says "I told you so, to me it was foretold"
For she seems to know the things you think, before you've thought them through
She says it isn't E.S.P. but just 'cause she loves you.

And when your life's at journey's end, with your family gathered near
You can give your thanks, to God above, for the ones you love so dear
And be so proud, they're marching in, to the new millennium
Looking forward expectantly, to the children still to come.

Great grandparents, and grans and granpas, uncles and aunts and such
Brothers and sisters, nieces and nephews, all love each other so much
Time or tide waits for no man, nothing stays the same
There's always new contestants in, this generation game.

SUNK WITHOUT A TRACE

**We know that once, upon a time, in days not long gone by
In the days of wooden ships and iron men along the Clyde
With riveters and caulkers, and plumbers side by side
Working, from dawn till dusk, or till the turning of the tide
With ship wrights, electricians, and painters by the score
We thought that building ships here, would last forever more
With building Queens, Elizabeth, Mary and QE2
It bonded workers closer, than any life they knew
Tea boys, foremen, managers, working in unison
To get a great ship ready for launch, maybe 20,000 tons
Everyone working together, each a helping hand
All across the country, in every shipyard in the land
From Yarrows o'er to Govan, from Fairfield's to the Elderslie
We never thought we wouldn't have those hands across the sea
Korea and the Japanese, cut the shipbuilding price
And built for magnates, brand new ships, for the proverbial bowl of rice
All over Britain, household names, we were going to lose them all
Stephen's and Connell's and Harland and Wolff, were going to the wall
John Brown's and Vicker's and the bigger yards, thought they were doing fine
But after Ailsa and Lobnitz, they would be next in line
With the choice being between Rosyth, and Devonport shipyards
We always knew that thousands of jobs would soon be on the cards
From when Brittania ruled the waves, we've gone right down the slips
We were once the workshop of the world, but now we build no ships
It is now flags of convenience, which sail around our shores
Great Britain is now a rowing boat, that hasn't got any oars
But we've done something Adolph couldn't do, with his great white Aryan race,
we've sent the United Kingdom, to the depths, without a trace
The U.S.A. now has the say of where Trident subs should be
I can only think, not on the brink, but at the bottom of the deep blue sea**

.Half turn for'ard. .Half astern. .Finished with engines.

.Log closed.

MARRIED WITH CHILDREN

When you've been 25 years married, it may not seem like bliss
So when you get a peck upon your cheek, it seems like love's first kiss
When you make the meals and tidy up, you feel like a knight so bold
And then you come to realise, its just that you're getting old.

She has you at the end of a string that only goes so long
And if you stretch it, she'll pull tight, and you're back where you belong
It makes you wonder where you're coming from, or where you're going to
Do you fight for change or accept it? You don't know what to do.

Do you agree with your kids telling you, the way that you should live?
The ones who only seem to take, they never seem to give
They'll ask you to do anything if it will suit their end
It's a crime to ask them, you're only meant to lend.

And if you're expecting back up, from your loving spouse
Then you'll find out, the kids come first, so you must be a louse
And when they are all tucked in bed
You'll find she has another sore head
And you shouldn't be such a silly old grouch
You should go and sleep on the living room couch.

Until the dawn , its light does send
Then your married bliss, starts over again.

PICTURES

Every picture tells a story, of people and places, and times gone by
And in each picture, diff'rent people, see diff'rent things, in their minds eye
For beauty is in the eye of the beholder, and having beheld, may see
A story, completely diff'rent from that of you and me.

Was Mona Lisa remembering, a life that might have been
Or was it places, people, or times, or lost love that she's seen
For life is just a picture, which, when enlarged, tells a diff'rent tale
When scrutinised or pondered o'er, will show in more detail
The love and trust and feeling, behind the wistful smile
That says, "how much I love you, won't you stay with me awhile."

The photograph of a new born child, held to its mother's breast
As she whispers endearments before laying the babe, to sleep, in its cosy nest
The picture shows, the bond that grows, the love that will never die
The camera catches the special moment, in its ever seeing eye.

A battle rages in a war torn land, far from strangers accusing gaze
The horrors of death, hid by distance, for ignorance to erase
But the camera catches for man to see, the evils, done in his name
Now people the world over, are witness in this, war game
The photographer keeps the film rolling, till he's sure, then, takes the snap
And the camera gives its final click, of truth, and it's a wrap.

GARTNAVEL (A.P.T.U.)

When you've been hitting the alcohol, and going round for round
Until you finally feel like, Sunday morning, coming down
Your family life is suffering, its now reached breaking strain
Instead of alcoholic bliss, all you feel is pain.

The A.P.T.U. is the place you'll finally attend
The care and help that you'll receive, will get you on the mend
Laurie, Ann and Kirsteen, Mike and Emily
Can help to get you through your day, with the aid of Anne Marie.

The other people who attend this place of quiet refuge
All have the same thing on their mind, to stop their subterfuge
To come to terms with their problems, they'll have time to stop and think
And come to realise its down to alcoholic drink.

John Barleycorn, has come to ruin, many a happy life
The grapes of wrath, have split up many a husband from his wife
And Usbehaugh has been the cause of children's lives to fail
And all because their mums or dads, have drunk too much strong ale.

If your preference is Vodka, Rum or maybe Gin
You'll find it just sneaks up on you, you're easily taken in
When love goes out the window, poverty comes in the door
You'll have to abstain from alcohol for now and ever more.

The next time you drink someone's health, and they raise their cup to thine
Then make it with a cup of tea, and not a glass of wine
If you drink super lagers, or Carlsberg special brew
Then you will do a stint at, GARTNAVEL A.P.T.U.

THE CLYDEVIEW BAR

If you walk down Yoker Ferry Road
Today or any day
And you pass right by the Woolbirn's Wharf
And stroll round to the bay
You'll always meet someone drinking
Vodka, Scotch or beer
For if they're drinking Callies
Then you'll think there's something queer
Like sipping a cheeky wee Beaujolais
And acting like a toff
For then you'll know you're sitting
At the alternative Woolbirn's Wharf.

A lovely mural now adorns the façade of the bar
And Postman Pat is on the side
He's down to have a jar
You can watch the Waverly sail by
And listen to the din
So long as you're not tempted
Just to dive right in.

There is no true proprietor
Or legitimate licensee
You make the hours to suit yourself
You know there is no key
Everyone in Yoker has come down here at some time
That's why I had to put
The bar down here in rhyme.

So if your drinking Buckie
Eldee or just a hauf
You'll find you're better spending time
At the alternative Woolbirn's Wharf.

THE FLOWERS OF SCOTLAND

**They say its just a boys' game, believe that if you will
But I've watched Cove Rangers Ladies team
And they won their games with skill
When I watched Cumbernauld Ladies, then even I could tell
They were good enough to go on and win
The Scottish Cup as well
The 14th of May was a glorious day in the year of '95
For the Ladies' Scottish Cup Final, really came alive
Cove Rangers or Cumbernauld would make themselves a name
McDermott Park just outside Perth, was the venue for that game
As the teams they faced each other
You could feel the sense of pride
That each side thought that they were, by far the better side
One thing was really certain, as sure as downs not up
The best team would walk away, with the Scottish cup
Cumbernauld opened up the score, and thought," we're doing fine"
But Cove scored from a free kick, just before half time
Then they went on to win the game, with such panache and ease
In the second half, Cumbernauld, came crashing to their knees
So now Cove Rangers Ladies, are on the up and up
Against the mighty Arsenal, for the British cup
Arsenal thought they would only, have to turn up on the day
Go through the motions, take the trophy, then be on their way
They only forgot to remember what matters most of all
The old adage, that we all know, (Pride goes before a fall)
Cove Rangers are British Champions, with points ten out of ten
For sending Arsenal football team, home to think again
Cove Rangers and Cumbernauld, are by far our better sides
For between them, they have restored our faith, and Scottish pride.**

BIRTHDAY WISHES MARY

I hope that you are having, a really smashing day
And doing the things you want to do, in your very special way
For you are a special person, with a place within my heart
That time or place or distance could never rend apart
You have a glow about you, like a beacon in the night
That comforts and reassures, and makes the world seem right
I know that baby Joseph, and husband Joe can tell
So long as you are close to them, then all is going well
I knew that you'd be perfect, as a mother and a wife
Especially helping baby Joseph, on his way through life
Through the years of growing up, you had that special touch
That's why those who hold you dear, love you quite so much
You have three lovely sisters, who are all with you just now
If not in body, then in mind, for they love you (and how)
You know I love you Mary, even though you're out of sight

So on this, your special day, for you, God bless and good night

Your loving brother

Eddie

THE SEARCH

I've spent a long time searching, for a guy I used to see
But everywhere that I would look, he wouldn't seem to be
I asked in all the places where friends would congregate
But the answer always seemed to be "Ed, you're just too late."

My wife was also looking for him, each and every day
But by the time that I'd get home, he'd gone the other way
So I'd sit down and rack my brains and really try to think
And just to help me concentrate, I'd have another drink.

First thing in the morning, I'd start my search anew
And just to help me on my way, I'd have a special brew
But just when I was getting close, and things were going fine
I'd meet another mate and we would share a Buckfast wine.

The guy that I was searching for, I used to know so well
But had he changed, or was it me? I couldn't really tell
Drinking 12 to 24 McEwan's export beer
Hardly leaves you feeling like, the laughing cavalier.

My breathing it was getting worse, my face would start to blotch
I know that I should never sit and drink too many scotch
Throughout all this searching, I became quite ill
So I had to see the doctor, he prescribed a little pill.

When the course of pills were finished, I was sober plain to see
I'd showered, shaved and combed my hair and I was filled with glee
The reflection in the mirror with a smile in his ee
The guy that I was searching for, was a happy, sober, me!

THE DREAM SHOP

The butcher's shop sells butcher meat, fishmongers they sell fish
The baker sells you nice hot snacks, the deli, a special dish
And if you fancy a curry, then the 'chinky' shop will do
But if you're feeling really cool, get an Indian vindaloo.

If you're with someone special, try Italian cuisine
And Greek food can be really nice if that is more your scene
If you go into a public house then that can bring you cheer
When you have six double whiskies, with a couple of pints of beer.

If you go into a clothes boutique, they want your hard earned pay
They don't want you buying M & S, but Armani or Versace
The jeweller sells watches and rings, till your money is all spent
But on leaving the shop, your purchases, have dropped 99 percent.

But there is a special shop, a shop that deals on dreams
And once you're in there you will find, that nothing's as it seems
If you back football, horses, or golf, you'll lose your togs
And if you do the greyhounds, then you've gone to the dogs.

You put your lot on the favourite, you know that it makes sense
Till the filly's unseated her rider just at the penultimate fence
You can tell how many punters, are taken for a ride
When you see that they've formed an orderly queue...
To the banks of the River Clyde.

If I could open a wee shop, I think it would be fair
To call it Ladbrokes's charity shop, and become a millionaire.

EDDIE

I love you more than words can tell
An old cliché you may say
But how else can I tell you?
I know no other way
I've admired you throughout the years
Despite the things you've done
'cos it was just the demon drink
That stole my fathers son
I remember all the good times
And the pleasures you have brought
For' in the past
There are so many
Memories to be sought
Your kindness, it astounds me
It has no limits and no end
Because to you
A total stranger
Could turn to as a friend.

I remember watching you from the veranda
My heart, washed away in a tide
I wanted to scream "don't go Eddie!
Just run away and hide!"
I was only a child
And couldn't see
Why you had to go away
Will I ever see you again
I thought
I hope so
If for a day.

You taught me how to play a tune
On the harmonica one night
'Wooden Heart'
I remember it well
Now I play it out of sight
When I think of you, as I did that day
My heart, it aches with pain
For you never meant to do those things
That got you put away

And still
After years gone by
Resounding in my ears
You never meant to do wrong!
You were responding to your fears.

You write poetry, so beautiful
About your dreams and fears
And because they're true
And hurt you
They fill my eyes with tears.

There's no changing the social hierarchy
Which first got you put away
You were born to be working class
And a fighter you became
You troubled every institution
You went against the flow
Right or wrong
When they demanded, YES!
You said "NO!"

So you've paid the price
For being…
A non conformist
All your life
You've got a good family
You have a great wife
But your life's been full of strife.

For me, its not YOUR fault
For the cards that you've been dealt
You broke the law
You took the rap
You gave to those who needed help
You had to do the things you did
Petty crime I'd say
Getting through life
Without doing those things
There was no other way

You've enjoyed life
Despite...
The problems you've had to face
The way you managed to handle things
Was with his saving grace.

You've lived hard
You've played hard (Kristofferson and Dr Hook)
You've gotten whatever you needed
By hook or by crook
You've boozed into oblivion
To forget the world your in
The irony is
Fate's taken a twist
Now its not just you!
The devil has got your daughter
There seems nothing you can do.

Young Margaret's life is hurling along
A collision course I'd say
Though hers is drugs related
Its similar in a way
It kills you
You can't help her
The pain
It is immense
But only she can stop the drugs
Get on the right side of the fence
For like a lamb
Who's wandering
On a dangerous country road
Before we know it
She'll take a hit
That will be her last LOAD!

You know how hard it is yourself
To make the change
Get it all to hell
Return to the devil
His booze and drugs
And stop living like a pair of mugs

If only I had the money
I'd take you both away
Just the pair of you
To a quiet place
Like a desert island, I'd say
You would help each other
Back on track
Perhaps it would work
There would be no looking back.

All your life
You've helped other people
Now help yourself
And Maggie too
You think you're nearing the end of the road
But before you go
There's one thing you should do
HELP YOURSELF AND MAGGIE TOO!!!

I love you!

Your wee sis.

ONLY FOOLS AND HORSES

Pat went down to London, where the streets were paved with gold
He didn't make much money, he just got bloody old
He became like Del Boy Trotter, to him that did appeal
Selling igloo homes to Eskimo's, now that's a brilliant deal
He sold sand to an Arab state (now wasn't that a peach)
What the Arabs didn't know, they'd just bought Blackpool Beach.

Paddy's biggest downfall, since he hit London town
He sold a girl (Diana) a tiara for a crown
He didn't know she'd marry Charles, but she did of course
Her tiara didn't fit her, and it ended in divorce
It caused a national scandal, Dodi Fayed died in shame
But it was Patrick Reilly who should have got the blame.

There was a guy, Tam Pepper, who was a lying rat
But everybody I know says, you're a bigger liar than Pat
If you know Pat Reilly, then you know he can talk
A hundred two legged Donkeys, now can't go for a walk
But Pat's a really nice guy, who wouldn't do you wrong
Till you buy from him a Rolex watch that's going for a song.

Pat has friends and family, who would always take him in
Until he needs a few bob, then they are taken in
But there is one thing I know, if life is really fair
Pat reckons by this time next year, he'll be a millionaire
There's another thing that I know, as sure as pig's can't fly
Pat always is, and will be, a really lovely guy.

So if you need a shoulder, on which you can depend
Pat will always try to be, a truly special friend.

Lots and lots of luck, Pat,
Fae your mate Eddie

PEDAL POWER

My brother rides a bicycle, it should be a velocipede
I don't think that he's into drugs but I know he's into speed
Because he is a pedaller, he knows his highway code
But he's been charged a hundred times for having a heavy load.

I'm not saying he's overweight (but you should hear his poor bike squeal)
I think he really needs one made out of titanium steel
And when he's getting new tyres, Good Year could do the trick
They could make him special ones about twelve inches thick.

He knows I get embarrassed when I hear people talk
That they saw Geordie Allan take his bike out for a walk
He uses it for errands and other household chores
But hitches on a trailer when he visits Lidl's stores.

Sometimes when we argue, I say "just take a hike"
But I know he never listens to me, he just gets on his bike
I know that it would probably, fulfill a lifelong dream
A big win at the bookie's shop, he'd buy a mean machine.

He wouldn't buy just any bike, oh no, he'd go to see
That other flying Scotsman by the name of Graham Obree
But that would be depressing, I would say "Och you've nae luck"
"You can bloody go and take, a right good flying f**k."

The only time his poor wee bike gets a rest at all
Is when it goes to Ladbrokes's shop and leans against the wall
Annemarie and Linda, and big Jen aren't lax
Instead of betting duty, they charge him council tax

Because he's in so often, he has to pay them rent
He tells me that is why his gambling money's always spent
I know you are three lovely girls, so please give George a hand
On a ten pound payout, add two digits, he'll feel really GRAND!

THREE Y.O. FILLIES RACE 12 FURLONGS
"NAE MARE FUR ME!"

Twelve runners are all going to post
But there's three with perfect form
ADNIL is the favourite
And second best RED STORM
SNAJ DELIGHT is no.1
And she's looking fine
I'll do a straight tri-cast
And have a winning line.

SNAJ DELIGHT to win the race at odds of 8 to 1
RED STORM finishing second, 4 to 1, go on my son
ADNIL coming home in third, an even money shot
A £20 straight tri-cast, the money's in the pot.

The flag has gone , they're off and running, things are looking good
My three wee fillies out in front, just like I knew they would
The race is nearly over, but something isn't right
They've taken the wrong turning, before the 7th flight.

The other horses in the field have seen the error made
And jumped the fence continuing on the downhill grade
What happened to my fillies? It was just a perfect snub
they were caught an hour later drinking in the Nag's Head Pub.

FEELING ROUGH

If you suffer from psoriasis, then you know its just skin deep
But some days that you go through, could really make you weep
It shows up most on Elbows, Ankles, Wrists and Knees
When people see you have it, then they can be a tease.

Because it looks unsightly, then people aren't sure
If you will pass it on to them, because it looks impure
It goes all red and blotchy, the skin begins to peel
When people talk about you, they don't know how you feel.

If you use coal tar treatments, then it stains all your clothes
Its just 3 months of torture, it gets right up your nose
The ultra violet treatment clears, psoriasis up quite well
You're feeling good for a few weeks, then its back, and you can tell.

Someday they'll find a treatment that will cure it totally
Then we won't need coal tar treatments, or even U.V.T.
I'll live a life of happiness, it will be pure bliss
The day they find a perfect cure, for my psoriasis.

CHERISHED MOMENTS

I was born at 24 William Street in November '51
The 6th child of the family but only the 5th son
Life was hard for my mum then, but she didn't seem to mind
For she was a lovely person, so good, and sweet and kind.

The first years of my life are blurred, but I know that they were good
For my mother she looked after us, just like we knew she would
Her family, it was complete, by the year of 61;
By that time there was ten of us, Ally, was the last one.

James and George had left the nest, in married life to live
To give the families they would have, the love they'd have to give
And so our mum she struggled on, with kids, like steps and stairs
Looked after us, and nurtured us, and chased away our cares.

Margaret was the eldest, in the house, and she became
My favourite one to talk to, though I was still a wean
I loved my baby sisters, enough to bring me to tears
And that love has never diminished, with the passing of the years.

In '64 my father died and it broke my mother's heart
I couldn't understand why, 'cause to me' they seemed worlds apart
After that, nothing seemed the same way in our house
There's a black sheep in every family, in ours he was a louse
The one thing that bothers me, for I just can't understand
How he's gone through life, when he isn't any semblance of a man.

Mary and Helen made the break and went to the U.S.A.
Now they and their families, live life the American way
I really am so proud of them, and miss them very much
But I guess its through my way of life, we just can't keep in touch.

Ally became a teacher and I'm very proud, you see
As well as being a brother, a close friend , I can be
Margaret is always with me, though we spend more time apart
But there always is a special place, for her, within my heart.

I'm bringing up my own family and don't seem to find the time
To spend with my brothers and sisters, if I could, that would be fine
We cannot go back through the years, to times we loved and knew
To my family, all I can say is, "goodnight, and God bless you."

FAMILY CIRCLES

**There is an old man that I've known, for more than twenty years
I've known him through the happy times, and also through the tears
Some people call him Mr. Burns, and others call him James
I've always called him Jimmy, some things don't ever change
He lost his wife ten years ago, or just a little more
But visits her most every day, his feelings forth to pour
She was a lovely person, on her you could rely
To lend a sympathetic ear, and never question why
Their daughter Catherine's married, and her husband's really nice
And they've made Jimmy a grand-dad, not only once but twice
The first in line is William, of whom they're really proud
And when he had his first child Liam, they wanted to shout out loud
But when wee Erin came along it really made their day
And helped compound the feeling, that such is nature's way
A nicer girl than Pamela, you know could not be found
If you saw Connor or Lauren, you'd see, what goes round comes around
So all in all whatever Jimmy and Becky started out
Has gone the complete circle, and come right round about
We know that life is what we make whether it be bad or good
And with God's love and grace and care, we know it always should
Its family ties that bind us, until our journey's end
We should always be prepared a helping hand to lend
You should always love each other, even though your out of sight
So to you and all your family, God bless and good night.**

To Auld Jimmy

Eddie

A LITTLE SPRIG OF HOLLY

It is oft with sprigs of Holly, we celebrate Christmas time
On December the second of every year, it will be with Holly of mine
For that was the day that I was blessed, with a girl so sweet and dear
And I'll nurture, and care for her, every day of every year.

Her soft blonde hair, and big blue eyes, her features lighten low
And bring to her face a tenderness, and loving trusting glow
To watch this child of mine grow up, just seems so sure and right
For even in this first year, she has made my world so bright.

I cherish the thought of her gran and grandad, watching her each day
Giving the same love they gave to me to help me on my way
And the love they get back in return is a blessing for all the years
Of the caring and sharing and laughing, and wiping away the tears.

I know that just now Holly can't begin to comprehend
That being her mum means I will go from the start right to the end
And as my Holly grows up, into young womanhood
I'll do all I can for her just like a mother should.

And even in my twilight years, I'll give thanks to the Lord above
For giving me a special Angel, in Holly, to give my love
With some ivy and some mistletoe, and a little sprig of Holly too
I'll give my thanks, and quietly say, goodnight and God bless you.

Lots of love

Mum

OUR THANKS FOR HARVEST DAY

We will reap the harvest, we will give our love
We will count our blessings from our Lord god up above
We will harvest crops of corn, and oats and crops of rye
But do we ever stop to think, of how and when or why.

Do we think of breakfast on our table and our plate
The dinner that we just enjoyed, the last supper that we ate
And do we finish of our meal by drinking grapes of wrath
Or do we drink the sweetest wine, by following his path.

For what we are about to receive, we give our thanks to thee
But sometimes there are none so blind, as he who will not see
Five loaves and two small fishes, he shared with a great host
That's why we give our praise to, Father, Son and Holy ghost.

To his apostles he gave wine, and then he broke the bread
And after he was crucified, he rose up from the dead
We give our hearts to Jesus Christ, for our sins he did repay
And for giving us the bread we eat, on this our harvest day.

WHY

I've believed in God throughout my life
When times were good, and through times of strife
But I wondered who should take the blame
On the day of the tragedy at Dunblane
Or the murder of the innocents in Bethlehem
When one babe escaped the carnage then
Or the plagues or famines ever since
The countless millions make me wince.

Of all the wars we've ever had
Since ancient times it seems so sad
Like the revolution in France, We'll say,
Or genocide in the U.S.A.
And the Russian stalags, were they worse
Than the anti- Semitic, German curse?

The Korean war or Vietnam
And the war between Iraq and Iran
The Falklands war was a terrible schism
As was Saddam's despotism.

Africa, India, and South East Asia too
Have all lost countless millions
But what is there to do?
The ethnic cleansing in Bosnia
Between Croatians and the Serbs
Surely the saying " The Holocaust"
Are the world's most frightening words.

The millions of deaths which are happening
In Rwanda and Zaire
Have we seen so much of it
We just don't seem to care
When will the Irish problem end?
Surely people could transcend
The list could go on, but I know indeed
Without divine intervention, we won't succeed.

Is God allowing us to erase
What's left of this the Human race?
If a nuclear conflict did occur
That would be the final war
So Dear Lord will you hear our plea

And let an end to violence be
Then we'll know those at Dunblane
Did not lose their lives in vain.

DONNIE GOES TO HOLLYROOD

Big Donald stands up in the house, to deliver his Oratory
He could make the tale of Frankenstein, sound like a fairy story
His opponents know they've gone too far, when he says "right now, that's it"
They'll find that they're being skewered by, his rapier sharp wit.

He really is a take on, looks like he's really slow
But when you catch his repartee, then its "Donald on you go"
He's been in politics now for forty years or so
Or maybe it's a hundred years, its only he who'd know.

Knightswood and Anniesland benefits, from him being on their side
Though he'll take up the cudgel, for most folk on the Clyde
A true gentleman and family man of that there is no doubt
And with him the Labour party, really packs some clout.

They say the clothes don't make the man, and I believe that's true
It's what is in his heart and mind that makes him close to you
Not for him Versace, Calvin Klein, oh no indeed
I think our Donald looks just fine, all dressed in Harris Tweed.

Tony Blair and Gordon Brown and others still to come
Will open the Scottish Parliament, for the new millennium
We can step into the future, fondly singing Auld Lang Syne
As a Scottish nation once again, now won't that be just fine

I think that you have done just great in politics and life
We can see a brighter future after years of tory strife
And when you go to Edinburgh, then you'll sort that out too
And the people of Scotland will rightly say, "Donald Dewar, God Bless You!"

9.11

Now a light has gone out, on a part of the world
As the Star Spangled Banner is slowly unfurled
And the pain runs so deeply, but voices sing sweetly
In the Land of the Free, and the Home of the Brave.

When buildings and lives are crushed 'neath the blast
Then surely the culprits will all feel the wrath
And people will fight for all that is right
In the Land of the Free, and the Home of the Brave.

We all know God moves in mysterious ways
His teaching's to follow for all of our day's
And "vengeance is mine", so saith the Lord
In the Land of the Free, and the Home of the Brave.

Now God fearing people o'er the world will unite
To follow America's fight for what's right
We will do what we must, for in God we all trust
In the land of the Free and the Home of the Brave.

CELEBRATIONS

**Everyone is gathered, they're here from far and near
From every corner of the British Isles
To wish a happy birthday to someone they hold so dear;
And to celebrate her fifty birthday miles.**

**For its Maggie McGuire's birthday, "hip, hip, hooray"
She deserves it from the start right to the end
And we all hope that Maggie has a really lovely day
For she's someone you're so proud to call your friend.**

**Its exactly half a century since the day of Maggie's birth
And its good to hear her birthday wishes sung
Its fifty years of tears for fears and tears of joy and mirth
She's not fifty years old, (more like fifty young).**

**Your Silver birthday came and went, there wasn't any fuss
we're here tonight to celebrate your Gold
in ten years time, you'll get a pass, to get you on the bus
its then you'll realise you're getting old.**

**precious metals seem to mark the passing of our time
to our children, it separates us from them
and like diamonds, rubies, emeralds, don't ever lose their shine
Maggie McGuire let us tell you," you're a gem"**

**you have friends here from the Emerald Isle who want to sing and cheer
though the singing isn't only just for you
they are celebrating Larsson, our footballer of the year
for he has passed his 'goalden' milestone too.**

So from every one who knows you

Maggie McGuire

Happy birthday!

HAPPY BIRTHDAY AMY

When Amy was born a year ago
It really changed our lives
Nothing before, or since then
Has been, even half as nice
For she is such a lovely little girl
Who really makes our day
And makes us think of our family
In the nicest possible way.

Nana Irene and papa Don
Give their love and tender care
It is so reassuring
To know they are always there
With their knowledge and experience
It helps to keep us right
Till Amy is sleeping peacefully
In her cot at night.

We know that, just now, Amy
Can't begin to comprehend
That being her parents means we will go
From the start right to the end.

And as our Amy grows up
Into young womanhood
We'll do all we can for her
Just like good parents should.

And as the years are passing
We'll thank the Lord above
For blessing us with a special child
Amy, to give our love.

And every 9th of November
In a very special way
We'll celebrate, and wish our child
A happy birthday day.

Lots of love and best wishes Amy,

Mum and Dad

LEGENDS

There are people no more with us who were legends in their time
Not least for drinking large amounts of booze
Whisky, rum, Jack Daniels, vodka, champagne, beer and lots of wine
Georgie Best is just the latest in the news.

Georgie had a special talent when it came to playing ball
You expected, every game for him to score
But it wasn't just at soccer that he missed the shout " last call"
"time gentlemen please, you can't have any more"

Jim Baxter will be with him, for he too loved a drink
Though he wouldn't stop at one, or two , or three
It was only on the fourth day, that he finally stopped to think
'Twas the big picture that people came to see.

Bobby Murdoch was a legend of the European Cup
But now we find that he has been Shanghaied
But he also was a legend, for the way that he could sup
And it broke our hearts when Bobby Murdoch died.

Andy Stewart played a Pibroch as the sun was going down
And the Scottish soldier's smile was looking wry
When they reached their destination, which was known as Campbelltown
Then the crew would drink the bloody whole Loch dry.

They would join big Lee Marvin o'er the alcoholic foam
They could swap their tales for all eternity
They'd be joined by Richard Burton, with a fine wine Jeroboam
As they sail across the alcoholic sea.

Dear old Ollie Reed will be there, as the Captain of the boat
Who else could be with such a motley crew?
With the world's biggest carryout, they couldn't stay afloat
So they'd go down with that good Old Mountain dew.

But now to finish off this Ode, I'd like to make a toast
There's some you win, and some you've got to lose
They were famous for their talent, that would be no idle boast
But more famous for consumption of the booze.

We will never see their like again, and then again we might
But if we did, we'd have to join their gang
We would have to drink for forty years and never miss a night
And when we're done, go with one mighty bang.

Billy Connolly could have been there, but the Big Yin missed the boat
He decided it was time to stop and think
If his career and family were going to stay afloat
Then he'd give up the bloody demon drink.

HRH, DIANA PRINCESS OF WALES

Diana was just a naïve young girl, till a princess she became
And all because of her love for Charles, who bore the Royal name
She soon found out, that fairy tales do not always end
(They lived happily ever after), royals have outlived that trend.

She brought two children to this world, and lavished love and care
On the two who mattered most of all, Her husband was elsewhere
She suffered guilt pains for the life she had to lead you see
And championed causes such as cancer, Aids and HIV.

In the middle of her (mines campaign), high profile she became
To help poor mutilated souls became her ultimate aim
She opened ordinary people's hearts and started a new trend
Instead of being princess Di, she became the people's friend.

So kings and queens of royal birth, take care and take heed
Instead of being heard to talk, Be seen to do the deed
Now H.R.H. Elizabeth, has come to realise
The steady hand of Britain may come off with second prize.

Marie Antoinette said of the hungry "let them all eat cake"
The peasants took her head, and now, no more she'll lie awake
Now Diana lies within her Isle, on the Spencer Estate
She probably mattered more you know, than Catherine the Great.

What matters most of all, is ordinary people having seen
Not Princess Diana laid to rest, but the funeral of a Queen.

THE BROONS

Granpaw Broon is the patriarch of the clan from doon Glebe Street
A nicer, wilier old fox you couldn't hope to meet
You know he's been a pensioner for three score years and four
He'll be drawing his pension for now and ever more.

First there's Granpaw, then there's Paw, and Maw and Joe and Hen
Then Daphne, Maggie, Horace, and baith the twins and then
The youngest of the family, though she's awfy quick tae learn
Tae everyone in Glebe Street, she's just known as THE BAIRN.

Every week since '36 the Broons have played mine host
To people all throughout the land, who read the Sunday Post
Their escapades at Stoorie Brae and doon in Peerie Glen
And even on their holidays up at the But 'n' Ben.

Dundee's most famous family have always made us smile
With them we know that we can go that other extra mile
It's family ties that bind them as you will surely ken
Like their counterparts in London, at the alternative No. 10.

Gordon Broon and Sarah, tend to be quite vague
Aboot the scamp that we all know, as Wee Door Wullie HAGUE
P.C. Murdoch staunin guard at Downing Street aw night
Tae watch Fat Boab and Soapy, and Wee Eck Dinnae fight.

All our politicians seem to think they're something great
They seem to think its they, who put our dinners on our plate
But I'd prefer the Glebe St gang to make up any law
The Bairn, with common sense, all the way up to Granpaw.

They'd have to hire Pickford's for the move to London town
But I'd love to watch Joe and Daphne, remove Gordon and Sarah Brown
Maw and Paw would have to oust Cherie and Tony Blair
Horace, the twins, the Bairn would beat their kids, that would be fair

With all the Broons in power, and that's including Hen
I reckon Britain would soon be a nation once again.

THE RIVERS OF BABYLON

**Doctor Jordan could you help me, I've been taking drugs and stuff
I've been taking uppers, downers, E's and H and it's not enough
I've tried eggs and coke and crack, and I've gone right by my station.**

Just try to calm yourself down now and take your medication.

**Doctor Jordan, it's Emperor Nero here, I'm trying to get home
If you re-direct my Methadone, I'll find my way to Rome
I started off as Stalin, it was just a hallucination.**

Listen Adolph, you just keep taking your medication.

**Doctor Jordan I think that I've OD'd. cause I'm not feeling well
I think I've had a bad deal, and ended up in hell
I had a word with Satan, and he raised my expectation.**

Listen you silly young Devil, keep taking your medication.

**Doctor Jordan, I want to come off drugs, cause I have a limitation
My dealer has just upped the price, 100% inflation
I just don't have the readies, and can't meet with the equation.**

No matter what the cost, you'll have to take your medication.

**Doctor Jordan, we don't want to have any kind of an abrasion
Perhaps Dr. Robertson could step in, as a sort of liaison
You wouldn't have to strike me off, in any segregation.**

You want me to make your drugs rehab, a triple assimilation?

**I would like to go along with the flow, but I'd end up all at sea
And my forename isn't river, but Lizbeth actually
I'm sorry to say, at least for the foreseeable duration
You're off my list, you'll have to go into voluntary liquidation.**

SOMETHING IN COMMON

I remember well Pat Devlin, who would ask you for the time
To go round to the chemists, for two bottles of V.P. Wine
And I also think of Martin and his brother Francie Hughes
Who would like to partake everyday of a bottle or three of booze
And then there was Joe Mullen, as a seaman he was able
He thought he could drink the rest of them under the bloody table
Wee Wullie McGuffie liked to drink, Whisky, Rum or Gin
What he didn't realise was, his time was drawing in
In fact most of the guy's I knew all liked a small libation
A part of the drinking heritage of this our Scottish nation
The thing they had in common, It's plain to see, is this
Each and everyone of them died, of liver Cirrhosis.

GOOD HEALTH TO YOU

**During a stay in hospital, I had time to contemplate
And realise that good health, is really something great
We take our lives for granted, till the day that we fall ill
And we have to spend a bit of time in our local hospital.**

**We feel really sorry for ourselves, till we see patients who are worse
Then the message strikes home, that ill health is a really terrible curse.**

**I was going to buy myself new shoes, as an extra special treat
And then next day I met a man, who didn't have any feet.**

**When things come into perspective like that, its then we realise
That health, not wealth, is surely the world's most treasured prize
It wouldn't do you any good to win the lottery
Only to be told that life would end for you the very next day.**

**So if you are in good health, then you should walk on air
Chin in, chest out and a good straight back, you're like a millionaire
And if you have that feeling, then you'll know my words are true
So I'd like to wish a long life, good luck, good health to you.**

THREE STEPS TO HEAVEN

If you follow the stairway to heaven
The first step you'll know is belief
For the calm that you feel when you get there
Will give you a sense of relief.

The hope in your heart, when you're taking each step
Upon each and every set stair
Shows that you are steadfastly going to get
Far above the floor of despair.

And finally when you reach your goal
When everything's heavenly bright
You'll be glad that God received your soul
You can bathe in his eternal light.

MARGARET

M.orning comes, the sun shines, the start of a new day
A.lways cheerful, hail or snow, for such is Maggie's way
R.inging in the changes, but always staying the same
G.iving, helping, sharing, seems to be the name of the game
A.nyday, in every way she can she'll help you out
R.ising to the occasion, of that there is no doubt
E.very cloud has a silver lining, her's is shining bright
T.hen just like Gladys, she'll help you to make it through the night.

You know I love you Margaret, as a sister and a friend
I always have and always will, until life's journey's end.

Your wee brother,

Eddie

THE 12 HOUR WHEELCHAIR RACE

The hospital staff are busy again, there's an influx taking place
It happens nearly every day, the 12 hour wheelchair race
They're moving patients to and fro, each to their allotted place
There's four in from the Western, and the Royal sent a case
But now it's medication time which all the staff like best
A small O.D. of Valium, to give them a good night's rest
But some patients aren't susceptible, and stay up half the night
The nurse's are run right off their feet, so something isn't right
9c needs a bedpan, and it's nearly 4am
12c just can't get to sleep, surely it's us and them
But now it's turned six thirty, and the sun has lit the sky
It's time to waken the patients up, and they all question "why?"
The hospital staff are busy again, there's an influx taking place
It happens nearly every day, the 12 hour wheelchair race.

A DOUBLE EPITAPH

On the Eighteenth day of June, Rose finally gave up
And joined Big John Thompson, drinking from God's loving cup
God decided John and Rose had spent too long apart
So he plucked the Rose and placed her, back in John Thompson's heart.

It was only one week later, that Alice went to look
And decided she would put her name into St. Peter's book
Although it broke her Husbands heart, John Lee knows he will see
His loving Alice once again, for all Eternity.

So John will watch his children and his grandkids as he should
Bloom and blossom, just like he and Allie knew they would
And when he's in his twilight years, then all the kids will know
That it was Alice and John's love, that helped them all to grow.

CARLA

Carla is a 7 year old, so happy and full of glee
In fact as far as I'm concerned, the loveliest there'll ever be
With her long fair hair and clear blue eyes, and pertly turned up nose
People comment on her beauty, everyplace to which she goes.

She fills her gran with love and warmth, in every single way
And makes her gran so happy, to be with her day by day
When she was born, even through the pain, my mind was in a whirl
When the midwife turned to me and said, " you have a lovely girl"

As Carla grows up through the years, into young womanhood
I hope that life is kind to her, the way I know it should
And if some day she marries some young man that she should meet
And look forward herself to the patter of tiny feet.

For then she'll know what her mum went through, with all the joy and tears
And appreciate, and give her love, for her happy childhood years.

THE ORIENTAL

I was up the town in Glasgow, going from there to here
And after paying the bills, I thought, I'll go and have a beer
So I strolled into a bar I didn't know was on that street
It's funny how you meet the type of people that you meet.

As far as public bars go it really was quite small
I could see and hear what was going on, no problem at all
Stranger's seem to sit alone, but standing at the bar
Discussing and debating, stood the regulars.

The patter was good, the music fine, the service excellent
The money that I spent in there, was money well spent
I listened and I noted what was said by one and all
On that street in the public house, called the Oriental.

The lassie who worked behind the bar was really very nice
A lovely conversation, sprinkled with a bit of spice
She liked listening to the music, all the sixties so I think
I enjoyed the company so much, I had some more to drink.

I am back home now to sit with my wife
And talk of the wee bar that entered my life
So if you're up at the town to meet with a pal
Then don't pass the pub called the Oriental.

Us westerners talk of what Confucius say
"Don't think about tomorrow, just take it day by day"
But if you feel a wee bit down, don't stop to think
Step into the Oriental and buy yourself a drink.

THE UNDEAD

The undead come from everywhere, from every niche and nook
Spectres, Ghosts, Banshees and Ghouls, and every type of spook
Though the cemetery is peaceful, at the dawn of every day
But when night falls, the undead, make it clear some one must pay
Crypts and Graves are opened, with the sound of silent screams
And innocents will be dragged into, the depths of nightmare dreams
The Bony hands of Death, will tear the heart out of the chest
And the Deaths Head grimace, stretched taut, there'll be no eternal rest.

VOTE FOR MORAG

**Morag's worked for Big Jim B
For nigh on twelve long years
The tales that she could tell
Could bring a grown man to tears
Big Jim works the oracle
In courts throughout the land
He's only brilliant at his task
With Morag's helping hand
Jim pled my daughter's case of late
She walked, and we know why
Jim's pleas of mitigation
Brought a tear to Christie's eye
"Impossible!" You might say
If you knew from the very start
That maybe Christie has a soul
But doesn't have a heart
With a nice line of delivery
And a bit of conman sense
Mr Bready adds to that
A touch of eloquence
But Morag keeps the clients informed
On everything to date
And gives a shoulder to cry on
When the tears come in a spate
My daughter thinks quite rightly
As Jim's secretary she's great
But I think her true vocation should be
Secretary of State
She's such a cheery person
Always ready with a smile
On your visits to the office
She makes them seem worthwhile
She always is so busy
Her P.C. is burning hot
From Margaret and her mum and dad
"Morag, thanks a lot!"**

DIPLOMA PAR EXCELLENCE

AWARDED TO

JAMES BREADY

LAWYER EXTRAORDINAIRE

**Jim Bready's a solicitor who's held in high esteem
If you're in trouble, he's the man that you'll want on your team
A mouthpiece, lawyer, legal eagle, call him what you will
I'd call him a perfect gentleman, well that is until
He stands up in a court of law and gives his legal spiel
His oratory and eloquence, can make the senses reel
"Well m'lud" you hear him say, and then he states his case
Before he's through, the Sheriff's caught
'tween a rock and a hard place
The P.F. sees his case begin to fail before his eyes
Instigating the proceedings, shows he wasn't very wise
The look of resignation on the Sheriff's face is plain
He doesn't want to see Jim Bready's face in his court again
He sums it up with not guilty being the verdict he must pass
With Big Jim showing once again, the law can be an ass
But with all things being equal, and if life was really fair
Jim Bready would be a Queen's Counsel, or even a Barrister
But at least he can go home at night to his loving family
Knowing that he gives his all, but what will be, will be
I'd really like to thank you Jim, for doing your very best
So to you and your wife and kids I'll say
"Good night and God bless"**

LOCKERBIE

It was on December twenty first, in Nineteen Eighty Eight
Two hundred and seventy innocents met a terrible fate
They happened to be travelling, on Pan Am one o three
Which was blown up by a terrorist bomb, in the skies o'er Lockerbie.

There were sons and daughters, mums and dads, travelling on that flight
No warning was ever given to them, of their fate that awful night
For the townsfolk living down below, on whom the airplane fell
That evening would remain to them, a living burning hell.

The world heard with shock and pain of how those people died
Surely such an atrocity, could not be justified
Protestant or Catholic, Arabic or Jew
Croatians, Serbs or Buddhists, what is there to do?

Where is the compassion that is taught within our faith?
Or does it only matter to those of another race?
We know it was mass murder, that took place upon that plane
But since then, we've had Omagh, and another town, Dunblane.

There must have been such floods of tears, from friends and families
To cause gigantic tidal waves, upon the seven seas
The pain and the suffering that was wrought, we cannot comprehend
We never have , and never will, until life's journey's end.

Was God asleep that fateful night, or did he just decide
That we could run this earth of his, without God on our side?
For if he did, then all upon this earth must know quite plain
That all who died will rest in peace, now and forever, Amen.

THE FACTS OF LICE

Midges always used to be the bane of Scottish life
But now I find that boogies, are once again so rife
When it comes to Insects, there are none that we hate more
Than the louse that sucks our children's blood, in fact it's all out war.

You can shampoo, cleanse and medicate, and then you think "that's it"
But it will take more than that to eradicate the common nit
It will take you time and patience, that's a fact and not a hunch
You have to hit those little Lice with a special sucker punch.

It starts off life as a little egg, which becomes a parasite
That multiplies by living on the head of your wee mite
To get rid of them, parents have to work in synchronisation
It's the only way to rid ourselves, of this lousy infestation.

If we could all start the treatment, working as a team
Whether we're using vinegar, or medicated cream
As parents or guardians, we have to learn, we have to pull our weight
To get those boogies, lice or nits, off of our Childs pate.

In the next two weeks or so, I hope that we will see
St. Brendan's school is once again, HEAD, infestation free.

P.S. That doesn't mean we get rid of the head.

THE GENERATION GAME

**There is a lovely couple , who have shared wedded bliss
It all started out twelve years ago, I think with love's first kiss
Alistair's in employment, an electronic engineer
A job he holds in high regard, in fact he has no peer.**

**His spare time is taken up, as a Rangers football fan
He would go to every Rangers game, anywhere, anytime he can
Rose is a nursing assistant, who works in the house McNair
But she'd prefer doing something else, something different, anywhere.**

**They have two lovely children, and both of them are boys
And they follow their fathers footsteps, through the tears and through the joys
Now Andrew is the eldest child and smart for the age of nine
When he was born, his mum and dad, thought that life was just sublime.**

**And then wee Graeme came along, he's reached the age of seven
So the family realise now, that they're in seventh heaven
When the children grow to adulthood, and bring home to dad and mum
The girlfriends that they have met, and the wedding bells to come.**

**We know what goes round comes around, till the circle is complete
And history repeats itself, with the patter of tiny feet
With the generations still to come, we know one thing indeed
The generation game will include, another family (REID).**

FOREGONE CONCLUSIONS

As sure as the sun rises in the morning
Then the moon comes out at night
And the tide comes in, then goes back out
Of that there is no doubt.

As sure as the day that we are born
We then begin to die
And as night follows day, then day follows night
That is definitely right.

As sure as some people in the world are rich
There'll always be more poor
And someone's older and wiser than you
Of that you can be sure.

But if there has to be a winner, then a loser there must be
And lucky at cards, unlucky in love, that's a stonewall certainty
Every cloud has a silver lining, or so I have been told
And at the end of every rainbow, there is a pot of gold.

As sure as there is a God above, then paradise must exist
And if that's true, then there's the hell, from which we must desist
But as sure as there are the heavens above, and stars are in the sky
Then there is one thing I have to ask myself, and that is simply, "why?"

SEASONS OF OUR LIVES

Spring is the beginning, of the lives we have to live
Whether we are born to take, or whether we're born to give
But some are born with, in between, a little give and take
And make their way throughout their lives, no enemies to make.

The summer of are lives are spent, blossoming to grow
And forming new ideas and paths, along which we must go
Though some of us will choose the place our seeds they will be sown
So that later on in life they will be fully grown.

And now we're into autumn time, and know the time is near
As up above us in the sky, the stars are shining clear
And all around us little ones will start to show a trace
Of what it's like to bloom and grow, in the seasons' botanic race.

In winter we will struggle on, reaching for the sky
Some they will not make it, and the others will wonder "why?"
Then they'll remember springtime, with the little take and give
And know the difference that it made, in helping us to live.

THE VISIT

**Eddie Allan went to London town to see the Millennium dome
It had been quite a few years since he strayed away from home
He was feeling so elated though he didn't quite know why
It's because he was up above the town, on board the London Eye.**

**He and Pat went for a walk when they perchanced to meet
On the steps, just at HorseGuards, at the bottom of Downing Street
But Gordon Brown the Chancellor, they warmly shook his hand
For Gordon's the main moneyman in all of this fair land.**

**They saw the House of Commons, Big Ben chimed the hours
So then they walked through Hyde Park, and wandered through the flowers
Carnaby and Bond Streets and into Harrods store
To see the sights of London could take forever more.**

**Eddie loved his visit, he had a lovely time
That is why he had to put these words down here in rhyme
But he's glad his back in Glasgow-you can keep your Millennium dome
As far as Ed's concerned, there is no place like home.**

THE BRITISH ISLES

ST George's strength it came from God, 'twas a dragon that he slew,
And where it's blood seeped through the earth, a lovely flower grew
The flower is England's emblem, as everybody knows
No flower is quite a beautiful as the lovely English Rose.

St Andrew came to Scotland, and taught it's breadth and length
And where he walked, the thistle grew, with thorns for added strength
The lion rampant reared it's head and brought the Scots to fame
For courage and for fortitude, they bear the Braveheart name.

In Ireland they had Finn McCool, a giant of a man
They say St Patrick put him there, to watch o'er Erin's land
So the Irish took the shamrock as a symbol of their Isle
Now Irish eyes will always bless each other with a smile.

St David went into a land and spread the Bible's tales
The dragon was in the people's hearts, the land is known as Wales
Welsh voices sang in battle, their courage grew within
The humble leek would be the emblem of the peace they'd win.

But all in all these emblems that we love all the while
Are all part of the heritage of this the British isles
Together they give the unity of the United Kingdom name
Separately they make each land a Nation once again.

STARS IN OUR EYES

So now I'm fifty years of age, it's time to look ahead
You're not long here upon this earth but you're a long time dead
When I was young I used to think when I grow up I'll be
Better than Bogart, George Raft, or even James Cagney

We used to play at soldiers, or cowboys, riding out
The goodies beat the baddies, of that there was no doubt
The lone ranger rode on silver, to even up the score
But now we've Schwarznegger, who'll be Back for ever more.

Tonto was an indian who didn't need to shout
All he'd say in his own quiet way was 'Cmon get him up Scout
But Brad Pitt is the pits now, Charlie Sheen has lost his shine
They couldn't compare to Ollie and Stan, on the trail of the lonesome pine.

I like to watch Steve Martin, when his jokes come in a spate
But WC Fields or Chaplin were really something great
Dean Martin and Jerry Lewis were a very funny pair
And Bob Hope was a comic with a really special flair.

So when I die and go to Heaven then I hope I'll see
Not the stars that shine above, in our Galaxy
But all the Stars of the Stage that have ever been
Or made their name on TV or the Silver Screen.

ONE SWEET LADY

Anne's a lollipop lady, who looks after our kids
Cause we all know that motorists, can sometimes hit the skids
She sees them safely over the road so they can get to school
She stops advancing traffic, with her giant lollipop tool.

Anne knows that lots of traffic, can really be quite scary
She'll try to reassure the kids, but teach them to be wary
The green cross code is something, that every kid should know
Look right, look left, then right again, all clear, then on you go.

Children are our future, their safety must come first
In a collision with a vehicle, they'll always come off worse
At play, on your way, to or back, road or track, home, or even school
Always be sure to remember, the green cross golden rule.

To cross the roads at school times, we need a traffic treaty
That's why the lollipop lady, is always the perfect sweetie
We know that road traffic accidents, cost lots of children's lives
So use your Ears, your Brain, your Eyes, and learn to always be streetwise.

Epilogue: **DESIDERATA**

"Go placidly amid the noise and the haste, and remember what peace there may be in silence. As far as possible, without surrender, be on good terms with all persons. Speak your truth quietly and clearly, and listen to the dull and ignorant, they too have their story. Avoid loud and aggressive persons, they are vexations to the spirit. If you compare yourself with others, you may become vain or bitter, for always there will be greater and lesser persons than yourself. Enjoy your achievements as well as your plans. Keep interested in your career, However humble, it is a real possession in the changing fortunes of time. Exercise caution in your business affairs, for the world is full of trickery. But let this not blind you to what virtue there is, many persons strive for high ideals and everywhere life is full of heroism. Be yourself. Especially do not feign affection. Neither be cynical about love, for in the face of all aridity and disenchantment, it is as perennial as the grass. Take kindly the counsel of the years, gracefully surrendering the things of youth. Nurture strength of spirit to shield you in sudden misfortune. But do not distress yourself with imaginings. Many fears are born of fatigue and loneliness. Beyond a wholesome discipline be gentle with yourself. You are a child of the universe, no less than the trees and the stars you have a right to be here. And whether or not it is clear to you, no doubt the universe is unfolding as it should. Therefore, be at peace with God, whatever you conceive Him to be. And whatever your labours and Aspirations, in the noisy confusion of life, keep peace with your soul. With all it's sham, drudgery and broken dreams, it is still a beautiful world. Be cheerful. Strive to be happy."

Desiderata: *something desired as essential*